The Wisdom of *Les Miserables*

To Lindsay and Jay,
May you discover your own
wisdom within these pages.

Alfred J. Garrotto

" . . . moving, loving, and universal . . ."

"extremely interesting and full of thoughtful reflection"

"Your personal story illustrates that the feelings of parenthood are universal."

"I find your material challenging and far-reaching in its benefits. I was especially intrigued by your analysis of wisdom."

"I like the analogy to a situation in a fictional masterpiece."

"I look forward to more wisdom from Victor Hugo and Jean Valjean."

"What thoughtful Reflections. I thoroughly enjoyed them."

"really thought provoking!"

The Wisdom of *Les Miserables*

Lessons From the Heart of Jean Valjean

by

Alfred J. Garrotto

The Wisdom of *Les Miserables:* Lessons From the Heart of Jean Valjean

ISBN 978-1-4357-0868-6

First Edition

Cover art by Douglas M. Lawson
© 2007, Douglas M. Lawson
All rights reserved

Manufactured/Printed in the United States of America

2008

Published by Lulu Press

Nonfiction by
Alfred J. Garrotto

Christ in Our Lives

Christians and Prayer

Christians Reconciling

Novels

Down a Narrow Alley

I'll Paint a Sun

Circles of Stone

Finding Isabella

A Love Forbidden

To Victor Hugo

For Esther, Monica,

Cristina, Alvaro and Dominic

who inspire me

and

own my heart

❧

Acknowledgements

I am grateful to my Monday night writing group—Ron Borland, David Cole, Igal Levy, Veronica Rossi, Myles Knapp and David Marshall. The wisdom, talent and encouragement of these outstanding writers challenge me to strive for excellence, since perfection is beyond my reach.

I am especially indebted to my friend, artist Douglas M. Lawson, for permitting me to use his stunning work, titled "Val," as the cover art for this book.

Thanks also to my professional colleagues, the men and women of the California Writers Club, Mount Diablo Branch and statewide, for their support and inspiration.

To quote philosopher and novelist Walker Percy:

> "There is a strange paradox about writing . . . . There's no occupation in the universe that is lonelier, and that at the same time depends more radically on a community, a commonwealth of other writers . . . . As lonely as is the craft of writing, it is the most social of vocations."

Contents

PREFACE

Wisdom has suffered from short supply during the war-ravaged history of the past two centuries. That poverty continues into our own twenty-first century. This book is a plea for wisdom, not only in the public arena, which can seem beyond our meager influence, but at its very root in the life experience of ordinary men and women. If each of us can grow in wisdom—even a little—and manifest that growth in our daily attitudes and behaviors, we have power trigger a spiritual and moral revolution that will spread a balm of peace and harmony over our troubled world.

What is wisdom? In *Les Miserables*, Victor Hugo shuns an academic "wisdom is . . ." form of definition. Instead, he reveals its qualities in the person of his main protagonist, Jean Valjean. The story begins with a spontaneous act of kindness done to the former convict by the self-effacing Charles-Francios-Bienvenu Myriel, Bishop of Digne. In turn, Jean Valjean pays that gift forward in charity to the poor and fair wages to his workers. He risks his life to save another's and adopts as his own daughter Fantine's child, Cosette. He surrenders to the law, rather than allow an innocent man to be imprisoned in his place. He forgives and spares his lifelong pursuer, Inspector Javert. Often, he wrestles with God, Jacob-like, seeking escape from the demands of conscience, only to resolve in the end to do what is right and just.

Hugo understood the wretched consequences for marginalized people (*les miserables*) when societies fail to learn from past generations' mistakes. The author's interior life, fueled by faith in God and activism for social justice, gave his literary voice power to move readers' emotions and rethink their attitudes and opinions.

In Jean Valjean, Hugo provides a moral compass for principled living. He offers his readers hope that it is possible to exercise freedom of conscience, choosing right over wrong in a difficult, sometimes hostile social and political environment.

INTRODUCTION

The inspiration for this book came to me in the early 1990s, as I wept through the final scene of Boublil and Schonberg's musical version of Victor Hugo's novel, *Les Miserables*. From its darkened perch in the balcony of San Francisco's Curran Theater, my heart flew to the bedside of the dying Jean Valjean. Over the course of the evening, this fictional hero had moved me with his tale of conversion, forgiveness, and moral fidelity. I wanted to be at his side as he uttered these final words to his beloved daughter Cosette: "To love one another is to see the face of God."

That magical experience led me to read the unabridged novel for the first time and subsequently to deeper immersion in Hugo's text.

When the show returned for a repeat engagement a few years later, my wife and I saw it again, this time with our two elementary school-age daughters. I am not embarrassed to admit that tears flowed again from opening curtain to the final reprise of "Do You Hear the People Sing?" My own little Cosettes became enthralled with the story and the magnificent music—and have remained so into their adult lives. During the year that followed, we wore out an original cast cassette by playing it to and from school every day.

A marvel of Hugo's story is its universal appeal. Set amid the political and social volatility of France during the first half of the nineteenth century, *Les Misérables* is still, in the words of author Mario Vargas Llosa, "one of the works that has been most influential in making so many men and women of all languages and cultures desire a more just, rational, and beautiful world than the one they live in."[1]

I discovered in Jean Valjean the essential qualities of principled living. For one like myself, a Christian who is always in process, Hugo's protagonist embodies the core values and ideals passed to me through my religious tradition. From this experience, I conceived a desire that grew into a passion. What if I could spend some time with Jean Valjean? What might I learn about life, love, and compassion for the poor from this former-convict-turned-saint? What might I share of this gift with others?

I originally planned to identify and draw upon themes from the novel. I have done that. Then, I intended to create a series of philosophical-theological essays based on those themes. I have not done that.

A new dynamic intervened along the way, and I followed the prompt of my creative instinct. Having meditated my way through the novel, I found it impossible to keep my own life experience at a safe distance from the work. Jean Valjean's journey from living death to redeemed life led me to review significant moments in my history. Like Hugo's protagonist, I have undergone a series of incarnations that have made me who I am today. Out of this examination has emerged, in part, an out-of-sequence memoir. Each new topic became an adventure in surprise that caused me, at different times, to shed tears of joy and cringe from memories long dormant.

While writing this book, I created a blog where I posted early-draft samples of the reflections that appear on these pages. In response to one of them, international photographer and graphic designer Michele Roohani[2] wrote with great wisdom and insight: "I read Hugo's masterpiece in French and Persian (my mother tongue) years ago. It's amazing how Hugo's book is relevant in my birth country, Iran. Cosette, Gavroche, Javert and even Eponine are known to millions of Iranians! Jean Valjean, a hero. Humanity knows no country, no boundary, no color or religion."

From the beginning stages of this project, my goal has been to help the reader awaken memories, explore personal feelings, and gain insight through reflection on Victor Hugo's text. I hope you will identify with my joy and pain, but move quickly to your own past and current experiences and their impact on your life journey. To that end, I have included an interactive element. A set of questions, under the heading, "Harvesting the Depth and Richness of My Life," follows each Reflection.

Ways To Use This Book

There are a number of possibilities for using this book for inspiration and personal growth.

Individuals have found it helpful to read a Reflection and spend time with the "Harvesting" questions. I have left space on the pages to write directly in the book, if you wish.

The structure of the book is also well-suited for group discussion within small in-home or church-related journaling and sharing groups.

The Wisdom of Les Miserables is a valuable resource for leaders of human growth workshops and adult education programs. You will find ample material for the discussion of current issues related to individual morality

(*The Primacy of Conscience*) and social justice (*les miserables*). The parenting sections (*Shock and Awe of Parenthood* and *The Power of Story*) invite discussion of family relationships.

However you use this book, I offer it to you as a gift, with a prayer that its message will lead you to deeper wisdom and provide nourishment for this portion of your journey.

The book which the reader has now before his eyes is, from one end to the other, in its whole and in its details, whatever may be the intermissions, the exceptions, or the defaults, the march from evil to good, from injustice to justice, from the false to the true, from night to day, from appetite to conscience, from rottenness to life, from brutality to duty, from Hell to Heaven, from nothingness to God. Starting point: matter; goal: the soul. Hydra at the beginning, angel at the end.*

Jean Valjean, Book Thirteenth, XX,
The Dead are Right
and the Living
are Not Wrong

&

* All quotations from the novel are taken from Charles E. Wilbour's 1862 English translation from the original French.

IN SEARCH OF WISDOM

Introduction

Wisdom is difficult to define, yet every dictionary attempts it. Victor Hugo did not offer an academic explanation, but revealed its meaning in poetic language and the lived experience of his characters.

Elusive Wisdom

Wisdom is a sacred communion. It is upon that condition that it ceases to be a sterile love of science, and becomes the one and supreme method by which to rally humanity; from philosophy it is promoted to religion.

Cosette, Book Second, VI:
Absolute Excellence of Prayer

&

Reflection

From various modern renditions of *wisdom*, I have borrowed pieces and put them together in one statement that makes sense to me:

Wisdom is the ability, developed through experience, internal reflection and insight, to discern what is true and to exercise good judgment.

Let me share what this statement means to me.

. . . ability developed through e*xperience*

Becoming wise requires that I commit myself to observing the human story as lived by those who preceded me on this planet. Analyzing that great body of experience, with its successes and failures, virtues and vices, I need to compare it to my own unfolding story—my life circumstances, perceived problems, and decision-making processes.

Victor Hugo steeped himself in the history of the human condition. The fact that his political leanings shifted over his lifetime might be viewed—and would be in the contemporary American scene—as vacillation and expediency. I prefer to think of it as a reflection of his hope that someone along the political spectrum, at some point in his lifetime, might eventually "get it right." He understood well the terrible consequences for society's marginalized populations—*les miserables*—of failure to learn from the mistakes of the past.

. . . *internal reflection*

Based on what humanity has learned over time and what my own personal history and instincts reveal to me, I am called upon, at a given moment in time, to make the best evaluation of what I must do in similar historical circumstances. In other words, I assess what has worked in the past to my benefit and to the greater good of all—and what hasn't.

Although Hugo's personal habits and behaviors seemed eccentric at times, the author of *Les Miserables* possessed a rich interior life that combined personal faith in God and a keen desire to promote "liberty and justice for all."

. . . and *insight*

Based on my observation of history and reflection on its meaning, I gain creative insight to develop a plan for living a satisfied and productive life and promoting the welfare of those around me and the world at large.

In *Les Miserables*, particularly in the life of protagonist Jean Valjean, Victor Hugo drew a map for human living that, if followed, would create a more just, rational, and beautiful world than most human beings live in today.

The evil portrayed in the persons of Inspector Javert and the Thenardiers (innkeepers), and in the legal and penal systems of the author's time, is a model of *in*human behavior. Hugo plunges his readers into the hell of these characters and institutions and their modern global counterparts (corporate greed, genocide, inter- and intra-religious slaughter, domestic poverty, homelessness, displaced refugees, etc.). Where does the list end?

. . . to discern what is *true* and to exercise *good judgment.*

Experience, reflection, insight: these are essential ingredients in the search for and discernment of elusive truth. To the extent that truth is available and achievable, it leads me to sound judgment . . . to wisdom.

Harvesting the Depth and Richness of My Life

How would I define or describe wisdom?

_____

_____

_____

_____

_____

_____

_____

_____

_____

_____

_____

_____

On a scale of one to ten (10 being the highest), how would I rate myself as a wise person? Why?

_____

_____

_____

_____

_____

_____

_____

_____

_____

_____

Who is the wisest person I have ever known or encountered? What is it (or was it) about him or her that merits this "gold star"?

_____

_____

_____

_____

_____

_____

_____

_____

_____

_____

_____

_____

Who in the current world community would I single out as someone who is—or seems to be—"wise"?
What is it about this person that merits this assessment?

_____

_____

_____

_____

_____

_____

_____

_____

_____

_____

_____

What would I need to do or change in my life to grow in wisdom?

A Distant Horizon

Wisdom . . . becomes the one and su-
preme method by which to rally humanity.

Cosette, Book Second, VI:
Absolute Excellence of Prayer

&

Reflection

Charles-Francois-Bienvenu Myriel, the bishop of Digne, opened the door to Jean Valjean's new life with an act of extravagant generosity and forgiveness. At that moment, neither the saintly cleric nor his beneficiary could predict that acceptance of a set of silver plates and candlesticks would baptize the paroled convict into a life of extraordinary virtue. Jean Valjean responded to his "second chance" by taking wisdom's first steps: paying forward the bishop's gift in charity to the poor, just wages for employees, and paternal devotion to Fantine's child, Cosette.

Driven by a new thirst for compassionate living, Jean Valjean pursued wisdom with ever-expanding commitment. He surrendered to the court, rather than allow the legal system to devour in his place the innocent, bewildered M. Champmathieu (the misidentified Valjean). Often tempted by the pull of former habits and attitudes, he struggled with the unyielding demands of his rediscovered conscience.

Reviewing my own life story, I trace my finger across the ruler of years, catching brief glimpses of something approaching authentic wisdom. Getting there requires wading through a swamp of mistakes and cowardly actions. Still, it is worth the journey.

As a young man in clerical ministry, I seem to have said and done some things that qualified as "wise." How do I know? I still encounter people who approach me with words like: "I'll never forget what you said to me thirty years ago. It changed my whole life."

I want to respond, "Quick! Tell me what I said. I need it now myself."

Instead, I respond with a sincere "Thank you" and recall St. Paul's insight that God's strength manifests itself in human weakness[1]—a lesson I review with regularity to maintain balance.

Victor Hugo's novel has not so much revealed to me a direct highway to wisdom, as it has affirmed for me the "stuff" of which wisdom is made. Jean Valjean has taught me that wisdom does not require perfection. I point to what is, for me, his most puzzling and seemingly unwise decision: his withdrawal from Cosette following her marriage to Marius Pontmercy. His daughter could only puzzle and grieve over what she might have done to merit this sudden coolness.

Still living at that time under the alias Ultimus Fauchelevent, Jean Valjean awoke each day with the lingering terror that his true identity as an escaped convict might yet come to light. Inspector Javert had ended his own life, yet the escaped convict's ingrained fear refused to die. Should the dreaded "outing" occur, he meant to spare his daughter and son-in-law the social damage such exposure might cause them. But to offer no reason for this abrupt separation? And without even a partial explanation, begging an oath of confidentiality? Jean Valjean's imperfection gives me hope of surviving my own lapses of judgment. I can only imagine the desolation of hauling the baggage of a dark secret through life, as he did.

Who am I to judge Jean Valjean? And, what if his decision to withdraw from the young couple had been unwise? Mistakes recognized and learned from might be more productive of good, in the end, than safe and right decisions. Now, that's something I can identify with.

For me, as for Jean Valjean, wisdom sails onward towards a far horizon. As it does, I strive each day to close the gap, or at least keep pace—lest I lose sight of it.

Harvesting the Depth and Richness of My Life

When did someone make a difference in my life, perhaps
without ever realizing it? Have I ever told that person?
How would I go about sharing that memory?

_____

_____

_____

_____

_____

_____

_____

_____

_____

When did someone tell me that I made a difference in
his or her life, and I did not recall the occasion or what I
might have said?

_____

_____

_____

_____

_____

_____

_____

_____

_____

_____

_____

When have I felt wise in a difficult situation?
What details do I recall about the incident?

_____

_____

_____

_____

_____

_____

_____

_____

_____

_____

_____

_____

_____

What mistake(s) have I made that led to growth in wisdom?

_____

_____

_____

_____

_____

_____

_____

_____

_____

_____

_____

_____

_____

THE PHANTOM PROMISE

Have you had a kindness shown?
Pass it on;
'Twas not given for thee alone.
Pass it on;
Let it travel down the years,
Let it wipe another's tears,
Till in Heaven the deed appears—
Pass it on.

Henry Burton

൧

Introduction

Arrested again! This time, not for pilfering a loaf of bread but for stealing silver plates from the bishop of Digne. What happened next shocked even the policemen who had done their righteous duty and saw little hope of rehabilitating this ex-convict who acknowledged only one rule of life—survival.

The passage introducing the first Reflection in this book, "I Am Purchasing Your Soul," contains the catalytic action that drives the rest of Victor Hugo's potentially life-changing novel.

In this early scene, Bishop Charles-Francios-Bienvenu Myriel not only forgave Jean Valjean for stealing his treasures, but added to the unrepentant thief's stash an heirloom set of silver candlesticks.

This act of over-the-top generosity ignites the story's passion fire. It is central to understanding everything that follows.

What the bishop said that day rescued Jean Valjean from the less-than-human, nameless being he had become during his nineteen years as prisoner "Number 24,601."[1]

Jean Valjean spent the rest of his life grappling with the implications of the bishop's pardon and his parting words, which I refer to as the "phantom promise."[2] They haunted him through each change of name and persona, as he evaded Inspector Javert's unrelenting pursuit.

I Am Purchasing Your Soul

*When Jean Valjean left the bishop's house .
. . he could understand nothing of what was
passing within him. He set himself stubbornly
in opposition to the angelic deeds and the gentle words of the old man, "you have promised
me to become an honest man. I am purchasing
your soul, and I withdraw it from the spirit of
perversity, and I give it to God Almighty."*

Fantine, Book Second, XIII:
Petit Gervais

&

Reflection

To be clear up front, Jean Valjean had never promised anything to Bishop Myriel. He had not committed to living a virtuous life in the service of others. The "promise," if one existed, resided solely in the hopeful heart of a kind old man whose love for society's marginalized, *les miserables*, extended even to this recidivist thief.

In the bishop's worldview Jean Valjean did not have to say, "I promise," or even nod in silent acceptance of obligation. The bishop considered his act of forgiveness to be "sacramental," that is, effecting in the Self of the gifted one a reciprocal commitment. In other words, the bishop's act of forgiveness itself bestowed grace unseen and, in the case of Jean Valjean, unwanted. In the act itself, the giver and God struck a bargain. "I am purchasing your soul," the cleric announced, "and I give it to God Almighty."[1]

Deal closed.

Sandwiched between the deity and the churchman stood the reluctant Jean Valjean, now burdened with a spiritual and moral debt that would follow him to his death: "When Jean Valjean left the bishop's house . . . he could understand nothing of what was passing within him."

Hugo reveals the difficulty Jean Valjean had (and would continue to have), wrestling Jacob-like with this angelic bishop and the presumed "promise":

> This (incident) came back to (Jean Val-
> jean) incessantly . . . . He felt dimly that
> the pardon of this priest was the hard-

est assault, and the most formidable at-
tack which he had yet sustained; . . .
that, this time, he must conquer or be
conquered, and that the struggle, a gi-
gantic and decisive struggle, had begun
between his own wickedness, and the
goodness of this man.[2]

My own reflection on this passage leaves me wondering: Is this the way it is with love? Does the fact of my
being loved bind me to the beloved and to a certain way of living into the unknown future? Here I
grapple with the concept of free will. Doesn't the ability
to make reasoned choices separate us from the rest of
the animal kingdom?

Has Hugo exposed a flaw in our understanding of
free will? Aren't I free to refuse love, even to reject both
the gift and the giver and walk away? I've done it before,
to other people and to God. But, if Hugo is right, the
smallest act of love is so binding and enduring that I am
indeed changed by it. I am obligated to forward that love
in some manner or form, whether I acknowledged the
originating act, or not.

Every good deed Jean Valjean performed from that
day forward posted a payment on the debt of his non-
promise. All that followed in Jean Valjean's life had its
birth in that holy man who had healed the former convict's wounded spirit. The bishop had made it impossible
for him ever again to feed on the bitter herbs of anger,
resentment and revenge.

Did a voice whisper in his ear that he
had just passed through the decisive
hour of his destiny, that there was no

longer a middle course for him, that if, thereafter, he should not be the best of men, he would be the worst, that he must now, so to speak, mount higher than the bishop, or fall lower than the galley slave; that, if he would become good, he must become an angel; that, if would remain wicked, he must become a monster? . . . One thing was certain, nor did he himself doubt it, that he was no longer the same man, that all was changed in him, that it was no longer in his power to prevent the bishop from having talked to him and having touched him.[3]

The message that survives in all this is that love creates a binding promise in the recipient of that love. The easiest option would be to dismiss the idea as the poetic creation of a skilled novelist. Instead, I forego the easy out and consider the possibility that Hugo might have it right. What if love does in fact create an obligation? Some scenarios might help.

Parental love

It is unimaginable that the bishop dismissed Jean Valjean from his thoughts during the years following his encounter with the homeless thief.

In the same way, as a parent I am never far from my adult children, regardless of physical distance. As I write this, our younger daughter is doing a social work internship in Costa Rica. Through the magic of e-mail and a minute-eating phone card, we remain in contact as if she

were away at college. The difference is that I cannot easily rush to her side should an emergency occur.

I have no right to say to my daughters, "You owe it
to me to live an honorable life." Yet it can be said that
genuine love of a mother or father for their child contains the seed of all good works and loving deeds that
child will perform as he or she grows to adulthood and
beyond. This debt is not owed to me, the parent, any
more than Jean Valjean owed payment to the bishop.

The promise hidden within a loving act takes on a life
of its own. It resides in the heart of the loved one and is
paid to God (or however one might understand the concept of a greater power).

Charity to strangers

A dollar or a sandwich given to a homeless person
contains a call to kindness in the recipient's heart. A parish church community I am involved with has helped a
local charity to purchase, refurbish, and make available
an apartment house for families in need of proper shelter
and social services. That "no strings" moment of hand-
ing over the keys to a freshly renovated and furnished
apartment represented countless loving acts by many different people.

What about the recipients of that kindness? How
have their lives changed? Do they struggle, as Hugo's
protagonist did, with the implications of this gift for
their own and their children's futures?

Divine love

Many believing people describe their personal conversion—that instant of first experience of God's love—

as a jumbled mix of joy and suffering. Being one of them, I feel, as did Jean Valjean, the joy of being loved and the pain of blindness; the exhilaration of having inherited an eternal treasure, coupled with awareness of the fragile gift now resting in my undeserving hands. Contained within the gift of God's love for me is that same phantom promise to become a new person.

Each of us must decide for ourselves if Victor Hugo got this mysterious and pivotal concept right—that every act of love contains within itself the seed of promise in the recipient. If he is correct—and I believe he is—this timeless insight gives him a lofty place among spiritual writers.

Harvesting the Depth and Richness of My Life

In what way do I identify with Jean Valjean in his confusion about the bishop's gift and his own mysterious "promise"?

_____

_____

_____

_____

_____

_____

_____

_____

_____

_____

_____

In what sense do I feel compelled to live my life in a certain way, because of the love I have received?

_____

_____

_____

_____

_____

_____

_____

_____

_____

_____

_____

In what way do I identify with Jean Valjean's wonderment at the implications of his "conversion": "Did a voice whisper in his ear that he had just passed through the decisive hour of his destiny?"

_____

_____

_____

_____

_____

_____

_____

_____

_____

_____

_____

When in my life did I pass "through the decisive hour of (my) destiny"? How would I describe that defining moment? What gave me strength to take the next step forward in my life?

_____

_____

_____

_____

_____

_____

_____

_____

_____

_____

_____

_____

LES MISERABLES

Introduction

An 18th century song of the lower classes:

I do not understand how God,
the father of men,
can torture his children
and his grandchildren,
and hear them cry
without being tortured himself.

St. Denis, Book Seventh, II: Roots

Nineteenth century France did not invent oppressive poverty. The distinction Victor Hugo made between *les miserables* of his time and the poor of biblical times—the *anawim* spoken of by the prophet Amos[1]—is the melding of two classes of "unfortunates": the innocent poor and the imprisoned criminal class. The latter were considered to have caused their own misery.

Rather than give us a philosophical lecture on the fusion of these two classes, Hugo created a fictional character, Jean Valjean, who represented in his own person both the criminal-convict class and society's innocent poor.

He Was But a Man

There is a point . . . at which the unfortunate and the infamous are associated and confounded into a single word, a fatal word, les miserables.

Marius, Book Eighth, V:
The Judas of Providence

℘

Reflection

In the person of Jean Valjean, we live the experience of a working man (a pruner of trees) pushed to the edge of desperation as sole provider for his widowed sister and her seven children. In a final loving, yet illegal, act he smashed a bakery window, snatched a loaf of bread— and got caught. His punishment, five years on the galleys; five that stretched to nineteen.

The desire to keep his sister's family from starvation made him a criminal before the law. And so we have in Jean Valjean the "innocent convict," a true nineteenth century *miserable.*

Release from prison offered Jean Valjean no restoration. The passport identifying him as a paroled convict made him anathema in every town and village he entered. He wandered without hope—more beast than human being. If degrees of lowliness exist, he occupied a place at the bottom of the pit. His sole "freedom," he reasoned—to steal again, this time avoiding detection and arrest.

The French Revolution and the decades that followed had failed to lift up *les miserables.* Nor did any other of the great social and political upheavals of the nineteenth and twentieth centuries. The innocent poor are still among us. Victor Hugo acknowledged this with the same frustrated resignation that fills the hearts of good people of means today. He observed conditions in France in the 1800s and declared, "Is it not when the fall is lowest that charity ought to be the greatest?"

With these words, Hugo foreshadowed the act of love that changed Jean Valjean's life and charted his future as benefactor to *les miserables.*

For all his moral and physical strength, Hugo's hero was not a Superman, "more powerful than a locomotive," but only a man who lived amid poverty and injustice and battled them to his death.

Harvesting the Depth and Richness My Life

Who are *les miserables* in the world today? in my own region? my neighborhood?

_____

_____

_____

_____

_____

_____

_____

_____

_____

_____

_____

How desperate would I have to be to break the law to feed or save a loved one?

_____

_____

_____

_____

_____

_____

_____

_____

_____

_____

_____

What is my first reaction when I read about someone being arrested on *suspicion* of committing a crime?

Jean Valjean became a wealthy man, but he never lost his personal identification with *les miserables*. In what sense do I consider myself one of this class?

Raise the Drawbridge!

*There is a point . . . at which the un-
fortunate and the infamous are associated
and confounded into a single word, a fatal
word,* les miserables; *whose fault is it?
And then, is it not when the fall is lowest
that charity ought to be the greatest?*

Marius, Book Eighth, V:
The Judas of Providence

ॐ

Reflection

At the dawn of the twentieth century, four decades after publication of Hugo's classic novel, a little boy and a little girl—my future parents—joined the millions of European children who crossed the Atlantic with their desperate families in search of hope. They came, this wave of *miserables*, invited by a Lady whose open heart sang to them with greater generosity than most of the inhabitants of her land.

> *Give me your tired, your poor,*
> *Your huddled masses yearning*
> *to breathe free,*
> *The wretched refuse of your teeming shore.*
> *Send these, the homeless,*
> *tempest-tost to me,*
> *I lift my lamp beside the golden door!*[1]

To say that these immigrants arrived in America with nothing would be untrue. Those entering the new Promised Land through the gates of Ellis Island[2] had each other. And they brought strong cultural and religious traditions. They also possessed a work ethic that accepted even the most menial labor.

The immigrant boy and girl grew up and later found each other in Santa Monica, California. In the years following their marriage, my two sisters and I were born. We were poor, but the only indications I had of this were family stories of communal survival during the Great Depression of the 1930s and my parents' occasional inability to pay the dollar-a-month tuition at St. Monica's School.

Millions of immigrants fought for their country abroad and sacrificed at home during World War II. After the war, America witnessed and encouraged the integration and gentrification of earlier waves of European immigrants. Little by little, Mom and Dad and their generation shed the label, "down-and-outers"—our version of Hugo's *les miserables*. As they gained acceptance within broader non-ethnic communities, the naturalized citizens of my parents' generation yielded their place at the bottom of the social order to the longer-suffering Native and African Americans. Those tired, poor, and huddled masses had not received Lady Liberty's invitation. The fortunate beneficiaries of the New World's bounty abandoned these *miserables* to struggle for their human rights alone.

Today, as masses head north from Mexico and Central America, entrenched immigrant descendants and their second-generation children seem to have forgotten where they came from. We have erased from memory the Harbor Lady's welcome. Like early buyers in a new housing development, we demand a halt to further growth. I know. I am one of them. A few years ago we purchased a newly built home in a quiet upscale subdivision. The builder and city planners recently announced that our street will become a main thoroughfare to a new development in the lovely hills behind us, where cattle now graze in the spring and summer.

Secure inside our fortress, be it our home or our nation, we cry out with the rest, "Lock the gates! Flood the moat! Raise the drawbridge!"

Harvesting the Depth and Richness of My Life

How far back in my own genealogy must I search to find
les miserables?

_____

_____

_____

_____

_____

_____

_____

_____

_____

_____

Where would I stand on a proposal to silence Emma
Lazarus's voice by expunging her welcoming words from
the base of the Statue of Liberty?

_____

_____

_____

_____

_____

_____

_____

_____

_____

_____

_____

What moral and social justice issues are involved in the current migration/immigration question?

_____
_____
_____
_____
_____
_____
_____
_____
_____
_____
_____
_____

Where do I stand on the issue of immigration, as it challenges the social order in North America?

_____
_____
_____
_____
_____
_____
_____
_____
_____
_____
_____
_____

Justice Trumps Mercy

When the fall is lowest . . . charity ought to be the greatest.

> Marius, Book Eighth, V:
> The Judas of Providence

ℬ

Reflection

The above isolated statement might cause us to wonder about Victor Hugo's understanding of the distinction between charity[1] and justice.[2] Was he unenlightened
about the preeminence of justice? Did the great author
think to ask—as a corollary to his conscience-nudging
call for charity—why *les miserables* in France were suffering without hope during the early 1800s? Did he
consider where social change might come from? Hugo's
answer to these questions is found in the brief and most
public period of Jean Valjean's post-prison life.

The author tells of a man of "about fifty," who arrived in Montreuil-sur-Mer, a town known for its
manufacture and export of cheap buttons, clasps and
"black glass trinkets." The newcomer had "the dress, the
manners, and the language of a labourer." During a fire
in what today we would call City Hall, this stranger
risked his life to rescue the police chief's children. That
very night a grateful populace, including the civil authorities, accepted him as one of their own, without inquiry
into his origins and legal status. Whatever this newcomer
had called himself before, the people of the town soon
dubbed him "Father Madeleine."[3]

Within three years, Monsieur Madeleine had de-
vised a less costly way to produce the town's primary
export. His invention made him wealthy and brought
prosperity to all around him. It is at this point in the
novel that Hugo hones the distinction between the virtues of charity (mercy) and justice:

> (Father Madeleine) was able to
> build a large factory, in which there

were two immense workshops, one
for the men and the other for the
women: whoever was needy could
go there and be sure of finding
work and wages . . . . Father Madeleine employed everybody: he had
only one condition, that each one
be an "honest man!" or an "honest
woman."[4]

More than any amount of charity on their behalf, *les
miserables* of the region of Montreuil-sur-Mer craved the
dignity of honorable labor and hope for their children's
future. By the work of their own hands, M. Madeleine's
employees fed their families, kept up their homes, and
prospered as they never had before. He had confronted
hopeless poverty and declared that it would not continue
in his region as long as, and to the extent that, he had
power to eradicate it.

Sadly, this Camelot period did not endure, for the en-
trepreneur or for his workers. A former employee, a
young mother named Fantine, lay dying in the hospital
funded by M. Madeleine, who was by now the town's
much-loved mayor. This abused and broken woman
begged him to bring her beloved child, Cosette, to her
side. He gave her his word.

At the same time, news arrived that authorities in another town had arrested the long-sought fugitive, Jean
Valjean! By keeping silent, M. Madeleine could rest forever, a free man. His silence guaranteed continued
prosperity and justice for the people of his region.

Something intervened. Not the bloodhound Inspector Javert, with his narrow sense of justice that
demanded the severest punishment for every transgres-

sion of the law. Not the criminal courts, prepared to condemn even a false Jean Valjean just to close the case and be done with the hunt.

No, the obstacle to ongoing justice and prosperity for the former *miserables* of the region turned out to be the tortured, but by now flawless, conscience of the real Jean Valjean. His converted spirit forbade him to destroy an innocent man.

Jean Valjean returned to prison but escaped nine months later by faking his own drowning. Going immediately to retrieve Cosette, he devoted himself to the single-minded endeavor of securing her safety. To accomplish this, he retreated into a labyrinth of secrecy, disguises and aliases, through which he guided the child to adulthood. He never surfaced again in a way that allowed him to work for social justice in the public arena. Over the ensuing years, he did what he could to share his covert wealth with the poor. Of necessity, he performed his acts of mercy in secret, often in complete anonymity.

As I meditate on these events, conscience nags at me around the same issue: the proportionality of mercy and justice. I understand the difference between the two virtues. Out of charity/mercy, I put my wallet where my convictions and moral inclinations lead me. But, I rarely put my body on the line in the cause of social justice. I have an impressive list of excuses for not marching against a war I despise, for not giving my time and energy to homeless shelters, for not laboring in the political arena for fair and just immigration laws . . . and on and on.

Being most comfortable with the written word, I pen letters to my congressional delegation. I chastise safely distant despots and plead for the release of prisoners of conscience. I never pass a petition table outside church without adding my signature. Having little courage for the sword of justice, I pray it's true the pen is mightier.

None of this stills for long the persistent nagging of my conscience.

Harvesting the Depth and Richness of My Life

What are my current habits of charitable giving? What plan do I have for sharing my financial resources? Or, do I simply react to ad hoc needs?

It may be easy to recall instances when I acted out of mercy, but when did I last perform an act of justice?

To what extent can I rightly claim dispensation from the work of justice because of primary obligations to my family or other pressing commitments?

_____
_____
_____
_____
_____
_____
_____
_____
_____
_____
_____

Where do I find among leaders in the private sector and government, examples of commitment to social responsibility? By what criteria do I align them to the side of justice?

_____
_____
_____
_____
_____
_____
_____
_____
_____
_____
_____
_____

THE PRIMACY

OF

CONSCIENCE

Introduction

One of my primary fascinations with Victor Hugo's *Les Miserables* is its detailed attention to the evolution of one man's conscience.

Nearly two decades in prison had beaten out of Jean Valjean all sense of right and wrong. Nothing remained but an animal instinct for survival. Despite Bishop Myriel's countercultural trust in his fundamental goodness, the parolee's capacity for moral judgment lagged behind.

Jean Valjean's first act following the bishop's purchase of his soul for God was the theft of a forty-sous coin. The beggar boy Petit Gervais[1] had dropped it as he came singing down a path towards the stranger. At the instant Jean Valjean's worn-out shoe shot out to cover the coin, he possessed an enormous treasure trove— silver plates and candlesticks! Jean Valjean committed a despicable act, but who would judge him culpable, since it flowed from the still-fresh wounds of his prison experience?

As the frightened boy fled the scene, conscience invaded Jean Valjean's soul through the back door of remorse. The bishop's words, "You have promised me to become an honest man," spoken only hours earlier, penetrated the fog of shameful habit.

"What a wretch I am!" Jean Valjean cried out to the unhearing trees and rocky footpath.

So pervasive was his guilt that he spent the rest of his life doling coins to beggar boys, each of whom he considered a spiritual surrogate of the wronged Gervais.

This event marked the first of many bouts that pitted Jean Valjean against his conscience. These battles would be brutal to the point of mental and physical exhaustion. With each new skirmish, the resurrected thief grew stronger. He vowed to face whatever life sent him and never again compromise the legacy of the bishop of Digne, to whose undeserved kindness he must attribute any good that would ever came to him.

Compass of the Unknown

*Certain faculties of man are directed towards the
Unknown; thought, meditation, prayer. The
Unknown is an ocean. What is conscience? It is
the compass of the Unknown. Thought, meditation, prayer, these are the great, mysterious
pointings of the needle.*

Cosette, Book Seventh, V: Prayer

℘

Reflection

What is this unseen faculty we call conscience—this "compass of the Unknown," in Hugo's words? What evidence do we have of its existence? Hugo's poetic metaphor is of little help until he adds that "thought, meditation, prayer" are conscience's "great, mysterious" guidance system.

I grew up being taught that conscience is "that little voice inside" that tells us what is right and should be done, and what is wrong and to be avoided. Yet, who will vouch for my little voice's wisdom and accuracy?

Cartoonists portray conscience as opposing counselors camped on our shoulders: a white-robed angel on one side, a black or red devil on the other. The angel counsels good decisions. The devil's theme? What appears evil is, in fact, a doorway to happiness. No one chooses evil for its own sake. Rather, every human decision is made to achieve a perceived good result. There are infinite motives for murder, but each provides relief from some perceived threat to the slayer's well-being.

Though I may not choose a resulting evil effect, my deliberate decisions and attitudes set in motion the events that promote love or inflict harm. No parent sets out from the moment of birth to destroy a child's health and happiness. Yet, it is clear that some parents cause grave psychological, physical and spiritual damage. Others—I have tried to be one of them—welcome their sons and daughters and nurture them along the uneven path from childhood to adulthood. Though not a perfect parental specimen, I have committed myself to modeling for my two daughters the higher values of the human spirit.

While Hugo's poetic "compass of the Unknown" hints at the essence of conscience, his characters dramatize the use and misuse of this universal human faculty and the tangible effects of moral decisions on the lives of people at every level of society. By a process of reverse psychic engineering, readers of the novel can trace the positive and negative results of human actions back through the decision-making processes that set them in motion.

There is no better model for this study than Jean Valjean himself, who throughout the novel wrestles with his conscience to the point of mental and emotional torment. Time and again he resists the illusory good. At the end of each grueling tug-of-war, he discovers that redemption and peace of mind result only from doing what is right.

A classic example of this struggle between good and evil took place when Jean Valjean, living as a man of industry under the alias M. Madeleine, learned that the authorities had arrested a man believed to be the long-sought fugitive—himself. The misfortune of poor old M. Champmathieu—the wrong Valjean—had provided a way to seal the true one's escape from Inspector Javert and achieve full immersion into his newfound life of respectability and wealth.

In the course of one endless night, a host of demons vied to possess Jean Valjean. They screeched from his past and tormented body and spirit. Every human instinct begged him to succumb to their enticements. His darker side spread before him a banquet of charitable deeds that only his continued freedom would make possible. Go back to prison? What a waste of a wealthy man's capacity for good deeds! At the end of that darkest night, Jean Valjean relied on the only sure compass available to him, a guardian angel who kept watch daily at his side: the late Charles-Francois-Bienvenu Myriel.

> (Jean Valjean) felt that the bishop was there, that the bishop was present all the more that he was dead, that the bishop was looking fixedly at him, that henceforth Mayor Madeleine with all his virtues would be abominable to him, and the galley slave, Jean Valjean, would be admirable and pure in his sight. That men saw his mask, but the bishop saw his face. That men saw his life, but the bishop saw his conscience. He must then go to Arras, deliver the wrong Jean Valjean, denounce the right one. Alas! that was the greatest of sacrifices, the most poignant of victories, the final step to be taken, but he must do it. Mournful destiny! he could only enter into sanctity in the sanctity of God, by returning into infamy in the eyes of men![1]

We are fortunate people, indeed, if we have someone in our life who sees our "face," who plays the role of conscience for us. In Andrew Lloyd Weber's *Evita*, Eva Peron had her Che. Actor Hugh Laurie, playing the eccentric Dr. Gregory House (in the TV series, *House*), has his colleague, Dr. James Wilson. For most married men and women, an insightful, loving spouse—like my own life partner—serves this role.

Parents' vocation and greatest challenge is to serve as their children's moral compass, providing clear thinking ("thought"), inner wisdom ("meditation"), and a connection with their Spiritual Other ("prayer"). Children are at grave risk of losing their way in the world without someone to mediate—not manage—the process by which they make good moral decisions and live accordingly.

I believe that my own moral choices are making a ripple of difference in the history of the world. Is that difference building up humanity or dragging the race down? These are the high stakes of exercising my "compass of the Unknown."

Harvesting the Depth and Richness of My Life

How do I experience the struggle of conscience in my daily life?

_____

_____

_____

_____

_____

_____

_____

_____

_____

_____

_____

Who in my life—living or dead—helps me to keep my moral compass pointed in the direction of what is right and good?

_____

_____

_____

_____

_____

_____

_____

_____

_____

_____

_____

_____

If I have made moral choices in the past that I now recognize as flawed, how have I tried to "make it right"?
How have I dealt with any guilt that followed?

_____

_____

_____

_____

_____

_____

_____

_____

_____

_____

_____

_____

When have I ever made the kind of difficult moral
choice that Jean Valjean did—one that caused embarrassment, exposure, or risk to myself?

_____

_____

_____

_____

_____

_____

_____

_____

_____

_____

_____

_____

What role do "thought, meditation, prayer" play in helping me distinguish good from evil and make important decisions accordingly?

Go In Peace

Jacob wrestled with the angel but one night. Alas! how many times have we seen Jean Valjean clenched, body to body, in the darkness with his con-science, and wrestling desperately against it . . . . How many times had he risen up bleeding, bruised, lacer-ated, illuminated, despair in his heart, serenity in his soul! and, conquered, felt himself the conqueror. And, after hav-ing racked, torn, and broken him, his conscience, standing above him, formidable, luminous, tranquil, said to him: "Now, go in peace."

Jean Valjean, Book Sixth, IV:
Immortale Jecur

&

Reflection

It's no picnic, this business of living a life of integrity. And no better image of the principled life exists in literature than Jean Valjean. Look what Bishop Myriel's love had gotten him into. At one point in her life the Spanish mystic, Teresa of Avila, complained to God, "If this is how you treat your friends, no wonder you have so few of them!" Human history is filled with examples of ordinary men and women who answered the question, "Why did you risk your life to rescue a stranger?" with a simple, "It was the right thing to do."

As in the biblical scene of the temptation of Jesus in the desert, life sometimes presents us with opportunities to take shortcuts to self-preservation, wealth and success. "They're all yours—lock, stock and barrel," the tempter says, "just . . ."[1] Just what? Betray my marriage commitment? Look the other way while an embezzler steals from the company I work for? Take steroids to gain a competitive advantage in sports?

In Jean Valjean's case, he only had to let the legal process work . . . in his favor. So what, if an innocent man went to prison in his stead? I imagine his internal dialogue as something like: "Think, Jean, of all the good you can do in the world with your great wealth and your concern for the poor and society's outcasts. The man falsely accused could never in a lifetime perform the charitable deeds you can in a single month. And Cosette! What will become of her if you go back to prison? Surely this is not what God would ask of you . . . unless your God is a cruel one, indeed."

Who would dare to blame Jean Valjean for making such a decision? Only himself, as Hugo states:

> Finally, he said to himself that it
> was a necessity, that his destiny
> was so fixed, that it was not for
> him to derange the arrange-
> ments of God, that at all events
> he must choose, either virtue
> without end, and abomination
> within, or sanctity within, and
> infamy without.[2]

During that one tortuous night, Jean Valjean wrestled
with his conscience . . . and lost. Or did he? By identifying himself as the true Valjean and surrendering to the
law, he gained the one thing every human being desires.
"After having racked, torn, and broken him, his conscience, standing above him, formidable, luminous,
tranquil, said to him: 'Now, go in peace' "—in the peace
of mind and soul that only a life of integrity provides.

I have thought at times, "If only I could have it out
with the dark side of conscience in a single bout and be
done with it." Victor Hugo understood that integrity
demands rematch after rematch. In an editorial aside the
author reflects:

> We are never done with con-
> science. Choose your course by
> it, Brutus; choose your course
> by it, Cato. It is bottomless, be-
> ing God.[3]

I know what it is to wrestle with conscience. And I
have taken the easy road at times. One moral compromise in particular continues to haunt me after more than

three decades. It occurred when a colleague confronted me about a situation that she feared might result in damage to our shared work and team harmony. I cannot reveal details about the circumstances because of possible embarrassment to others involved. Unwilling to admit the truth, I looked her earnestly in the eye and said, "You're mistaken. It isn't true." But it was true, and I knew it.

I have relived that moment hundreds of times and wished I'd had the courage to respond truthfully and beg my colleague's understanding of the situation. No matter how often I replay that scene, it ends the way it did in real life—and I flush with shame as if it were happening in real time.

I have also known the blessing that comes with choosing right over wrong—counterbalancing, I hope, the weight of my failures. At the end of some long, dark nights, I have heard my conscience whisper, as Jean Valjean heard his, "Now, go in peace."

Harvesting the Depth the Depth and Richness of My Life

To what extent can I identify with Jean Valjean's struggle to live a life of integrity and fidelity to his better self?

_____

_____

_____

_____

_____

_____

_____

_____

_____

_____

_____

_____

How would I describe the peace of mind and soul I have felt after making what I knew to be a right decision— one that honored the best yearning of my inner Self?

_____

_____

_____

_____

_____

_____

_____

_____

_____

_____

_____

_____

What moral decision haunts me from my past?
How have I made peace with that decision?
If I am still troubled by it, what can I do to put it to rest?

The Violence of Thought

*One of (Inspector Javert's) causes of anxiety
was that he was compelled to think. The very
violence of . . . contradictory emotions forced
him to it.*

Jean Valjean, Book Fourth, I:
Javert Off the Track

છ

Reflection

With an act of unconditional generosity Bishop Myriel had claimed Jean Valjean's soul for God. At first, the former convict railed against his unwelcome debt. Unable to escape it, he succumbed. In what is the most famous and remarkable conversion story in all of fiction, Jean Valjean transformed himself into the quintessential honorable man.

It shakes me when I encounter an idea, behavior or event whose source is beyond the limits of my worldview. Whatever its source, it catches me off guard. A spiritual-moral earthquake unsettles what Paul Tillich called the "ground of our being."

My first adult experience of freely given love triggered in me great emotional and intellectual turbulence. Its origin? The generous heart of another human being who took the risk of declaring herself. How was I to respond? At the time, I believed this kind of love existed only for others, not for me. The suddenness of it caused the soles of my feet to lose contact with the ground. Being a Roman Catholic priest, I had committed myself to a life of celibacy. I understood my vocation as a mandate to love *all* of God's people. I had promised not to let myself love or be loved by one person in an intimate, human way—as if I had power to deflect or deny the experience. The newness of being cherished simply for myself challenged all the rules I had established for the governance of my life.

The ultimate test of Jean Valjean's conversion occurred at the barricades in the streets of Paris during a student uprising in 1832. The insurgents had identified the policeman Javert as a spy and taken him prisoner.

Those brave and foolish men and women, who themselves had only hours left to breathe the air of their beloved France, condemned the policeman to die. With a Myriel-like plan in mind, the old ex-convict volunteered to carry out the execution. Instead, he spared his stalker's life.

Now, the baton passed to Javert. His turn had come at last to deal with a demonstration of unconditional compassion. Nothing in his narrow life had prepared him for it. As the bishop had purchased a paroled convict's soul for God, Jean Valjean had just purchased Inspector Javert's. The prospect of reorganizing his priorities caused the policeman unspeakable confusion and suffering. Victor Hugo describes this wretched man's turmoil:

> Thought, an unaccustomed thing to (him), and singularly painful . . . . Thought, upon any subject, no matter what, outside of the narrow circle of his functions, had been to him, in all cases, a folly and a fatigue; but thought upon the day which had just gone by, was torture. He must absolutely, however, look into his conscience after such shocks, and render an account of himself to himself.[1]

And what did Javert discover in the dusty cellars of his conscience? Gratitude for the gift of his life? Regret for his many transgressions committed in the name of the Law? In the darkness of his inmost self, he found only shame for allowing himself to be indebted to a criminal he had hunted down the years with self-righteous determination.

I can identify with the bewildered inspector. Love rushed at me with such violence that I was, in Hugo's words, "compelled to think." What a life-altering concept—that love can ignite the intellect and impose itself by force upon the human spirit! And so began my journey towards fuller intellectual and emotional integrity—reassessment of my self-identity, my purpose and place in the universe. Having tasted the generosity of intimate human love, I could never be the same again.

Thought can be violent. My psycho-spiritual structure has quaked like the shifting California earth before the compulsion to think sensibly about my life choices. Unlike Javert I do not find an enemy in reason. I have chosen Jean Valjean's path of hopeful engagement with rationality, conscience and faith.

Harvesting the Depth and Richness of My Life

Who has purchased my soul with the currency of love?

_____
_____
_____
_____
_____
_____
_____
_____
_____
_____
_____
_____

What landmark events of my life have shaken "the ground of my being" and caused me to rethink long-held assumptions?

_____
_____
_____
_____
_____
_____
_____
_____
_____
_____
_____
_____

When have I felt "compelled to think," whether I wanted to examine my life, or not?

_____
_____
_____
_____
_____
_____
_____
_____
_____
_____
_____
_____

When and how did my positive response to unselfish love change the course of my life?

_____
_____
_____
_____
_____
_____
_____
_____
_____
_____
_____

MY NAME IS
JEAN VALJEAN

*A name is a centre; a deep
assimilation.*

St. Denis, Book Seventh, II:
Roots

*Names acquire their own life and drag the
person on their own path for their own
reasons, which we can't know.*

Louise Erdrich,
Four Souls

૱

A Name Too Small

To teach Cosette to read, and to watch her playing, was nearly all Jean Valjean's life. And then, he would talk about her mother, and teach her to pray.

Cosette, Book Fourth, III:
Two Misfortunes Mingled
Make Happiness

෫ට

Reflection

Ever the cautious escapee, alert to Inspector Javert's pursuit, Jean Valjean thought it best not reveal the name of Cosette's mother for the child's own protection. Perhaps he could not bear the possibility that Cosette might trace her mother's path. What if Cossette learned of her rapid slide from the freshness of young womanhood to a hag who sold her teeth, hair, and finally her body to pay her room and board? As children often do, Cosette might have blamed herself for her mother's suffering. In this swirl of conflicting human motivations, Jean Valjean spared Cosette the details of Fantine's lost innocence and doomed struggle to provide for her child.

To demonstrate the importance and inadequacy of names, scientist-cosmologist Brian Swimme[1] does not use the term "God" to speak of the benevolent, guiding force in the universe. He considers the label too limiting for such a being.

Perhaps Jean Valjean considered the diminutive form, Fantine, too small to encompass the essence of his beloved. Rather than limit her vital force by attaching a name to Cosette's mother, he chose—rightly or wrongly —to leave the name unspoken, even to the child. The tender heart of Jean Valjean intuited that absence of the name served as the only adequate expression of the complex, sacrificial nature of this woman who epitomized *les miserables.*

Fantine had left behind in death a daughter she could no longer support and an impossible debt owed to the heartless innkeepers, the Thenardiers. To the kindly M. Madeleine she owed the dignity of her last days on earth and the hope of her daughter's return.

If Jean Valjean awaited that elusive "perfect moment" when Cosette could receive this gift of her mother's name as the wondrous blessing it had been for him, it would soon be too late. She had asked him many times over the years, but with the same result:

> Whenever (Cosette) happened to ask Jean Valjean what it was, Jean Valjean was silent. If she repeated her question, he answered by a smile; the smile ended with a tear. This silence of Jean Valjean's covered Fantine with night.[2]

Only on his deathbed, did he finally declare:

> The time has come for me to tell you the name of your mother. Her name was Fantine. Remember that name: Fantine. Fall on your knees whenever you pronounce it. She suffered much. And loved you much.[3]

To die withholding this sacred gift from Cosette might result in Fantine's name being lost forever.

Harvesting the Depth and Richness of My Life

What kinds of personal information about myself or my
past history have I withheld from my children?
or about their past? Why do I consider this necessary?

When have I been in a situation (other than legal) where
withholding a person's name and personal information
seemed the best choice?

A Name is a Centre

*. . . all his life was effaced, even
to his name. He was no longer Jean Valjean: he was Number 24,601.*

Fantine, Book Second, VI:
Jean Valjean

છૐ

Reflection

Shakespeare's Juliet asked her beloved, "What's in a name?"[1] Two hundred years later, Victor Hugo responded: "A name is a centre; a deep assimilation."[2]

No wonder parents take such care in choosing their child's name. Who doesn't at least consult a "baby's name" book or online service, even if just to learn its root meaning? John, for example, has strong biblical association ("God has been gracious"; "God has shown favor"). It calls to mind a well-groomed, intelligent man who is solid and dependable.

Almost nothing imposed from the outside is more closely allied with our selfhood than our name. It follows us through all phases and stages of life. Engraved on a headstone, a name reminds the living that it resides on earth long after its bearer has departed. Knowing this, we impose a name on a newborn or change the name of an adopted child before we ever know who this person is, what decisions and events will define his or her existence, or the place the child is destined to occupy in human history.

Names can define us in the eyes of others. Calling a male child Brock propels him into a solid, masculine self-image. Chauncey, on the other hand, might sentence an Anglo-American boy to years of struggle for acceptance in school, athletics, and the business world.

Gods worshiped in ancient civilizations bore names corresponding to their perceived powers and mission in the galaxy of divine beings. Moses, a believer in the one God of his ancestors, heard a mysterious voice at the site of a burning bush. He did what I would do now. He asked for some form of ID:

> "Suppose I go to the People of Israel and I tell them, 'The God of your fathers sent me to you'; and they ask me, 'What is his name?' What do I tell them?"[3] The voice responded in effect, "I am 'Nameless' " (that is, "I-AM-WHO-I-AM" or, "I am 'being,' pure and simple.").[4]

With this, the voice in the bush declared its self-image: I am beyond the limitations of a label. Faith traditions that cherish the Christian and/or Hebrew Scriptures cling to the sacredness of each person's name. God assured the people of Israel through the prophet Isaiah:

> Don't be afraid. I've redeemed you.
> I've called your name. You're mine.[5]

These words applied originally to the whole people of Israel, but subsequent believers have personalized their intent: "Wow! God knows *my* name." Jesus echoed this intimate relationship between God and each human being, saying:

> What's the price of a pet canary? Some loose change, right? And God cares what happens to it even more than you do. He pays even greater attention to you, down to the last detail—even numbering the hairs of your head. So don't be intimidated by all this bully talk. You're worth more than a million canaries.[6]

Children—parents too, sometimes—get lost in the plain sight of family structures. This is a common lament of children and taken-for-granted wives/moms, husbands/dads. How does it happen that we can even become invisible within our worshiping communities, where unconditional love and respect are professed as prime values.

For years I felt adrift within the bureaucratic structure of a mammoth Roman Catholic diocese. Throughout my years of training, I had heard—and believed—the mantra, "The Church will take care you." After several years of ministry, it became clear that those in whom I had placed my trust considered me an "it," not a "thou."[7] They didn't even know my name! I felt like a game board piece being moved from parish to parish without consultation or concern for my unique personhood or ministerial gifts. Having lived too long with the unfulfilled promise of fraternal equality, I took charge of my life. I began making healthier decisions about my ministerial path.

"A name is a centre; a deep assimilation."

Depriving a human being of a name disengages that person from the core of his or her being. No wonder punitive societies assign numbers to their convicts. The perversity of this practice goes beyond administrative procedure. It aims to destroy the prisoner's sense of Self.

"He was no longer Jean Valjean: he was Number 24,601."[8] With these words, Victor Hugo gave poignant expression to his protagonist's descent into hell.

Harvesting the Depth and Richness of My Life

When have I felt like little more than a number, lost in the crowd of people with whom I live, work, socialize?

_____

_____

_____

_____

_____

_____

_____

_____

_____

_____

If I am a parent, by what process did I/we name my/our child(ren)?

_____

_____

_____

_____

_____

_____

_____

_____

_____

_____

_____

How well does the name of each of my children fit the emerging person? What evidence supports my answer?

A Name is a Me

My name is Jean Valjean. I am a convict; I have been nineteen years in the galleys.

Fantine, Book Second, III:
The Heroism of Passive Obedience

ॐ

Reflection

The psychology and spirituality of names fascinate me. Deprived of the last thread of dignity as a slave in the national penal system, the newly released prisoner found himself at the door of last resort, that of the bishop of Digne. Known for the past nineteen years as convict 24,601, the parolee asked for bread and shelter for the night.[1] Nothing more. With shame he confessed that even the animal world had rejected him: "I crept into a dog kennel, the dog bit me, and drove me away."

Then, in a moment of resurrected self-respect, the beggar reclaimed the last remnant of humanity that the penal system had stripped away: "My name is Jean Valjean." With this affirmation, the parolee declared that his life in prison may have labeled him, but it did not and would never define him. Sadly, the ripped cloth of resurrected self-identity proved short-lived. Circumstances soon required Jean Valjean to disguise himself with sequential aliases, including M. Madeleine and Ultimus Fauchelevent, "brother" of the old gardener[2] at the cloistered convent of The Petit Picpus.[3]

He wore his assumed names and their accompanying disguises like costume changes. They never rested easily upon his spirit. He lived apart from society and caused his blossoming daughter to do so—for her own protection—until he could no longer restrain the yearnings of Cosette's heart for young Marius Pontmercy.

Only at the end of Jean Valjean's life, with the dreaded Inspector Javert no longer a threat, did he feel secure enough to unveil his birth name and own it once again. The former convict had arrived at a moment of conscience-clearing, deathbed honesty.[4]

> "Fauchelevent lent me his name in vain," he revealed to the young couple. "I had no right to make use of it; he could give it to me, I could not take it. A name is a Me. To purloin a name, and to put yourself under it, is dishonest. The letters of the alphabet may be stolen as well as a purse or a watch . . . . To live I once stole a loaf of bread; today, to live, I will not steal a name."[5]

I have long had questions about my own name. Uppermost is whether Alfred Joseph encompasses the "Me" that Victor Hugo speaks of. I have wondered what my Creator calls me. My first and middle names? Or, am I known and called by some other name? If God holds me in eternal thought under a different name, what might it be? Fortunately, I have lived long enough to gain some insight about my essence-name, my Me.

Alfred has never rested comfortably upon my sense of Self. It might as well be Marius or Ultimus. I inherited ("purloined"?) this name from my paternal grandfather, Alfredo (Alfio in its Sicilian form) whom I never knew.

My middle name is Joseph, a better fit, and I understand why some people go by "Initial, Middle Name, Surname," such as A. Joseph, which I never have.[6] My late parents were Joseph and Josephine,[7] named after the husband of Mary of Nazareth, earth-father of Jesus of Nazareth. Joseph has tight association in Christian tradition with parenthood.

From early childhood, I yearned to become a priest —a capital-F Father. I confess that, at first, Father Garrotto had more significance to me as a title of status and respect in both church and civic society, than its spiritual meaning. It took me a number of years to grow into an awareness of my role as "father to all."

For eighteen years I lived under the title "Father" or, to many, "Father Al." Over time I grew into the spiritual parenthood the title implied. This became most vivid to me when baptizing infants and adults into a new life in Christ and when reconciling penitents to their better selves and to the community they had wounded.

Then, something happened.

I experienced a dawning and uncomfortable sense of being called to something new. To what, I did not know. In the 1970s we called it a midlife crisis, but for me it had deeper significance. I set aside the capital-F title and withdrew from active ministry. Two years later, at 46, I married, but declared myself too old for parenthood. I had grown too set in my ways to endure the disruption I had witnessed in the lives of men younger and more energetic than I.

How can I explain why in my early fifties I agreed to not one but two adoptions? How, except to admit that the "something new" I had sought earlier was not a different Me but a different form of my personhood, one that had been evolving throughout my adult life. From a capital-F Father I evolved into a lowercase-f father and could not imagine doing anything else with my life. Who am I, then? Who am I at that essence-place where I experience, as Victor Hugo indicates, my Me?

I have become Joseph—father. It is the fulfillment of a destiny bestowed at birth—perhaps before. Further-

more, I discovered that this evolutionary change represented, not a sudden break from my life path, but a
continuum along the single timeline of my years.

Hugo tells us that, in the end, Jean Valjean cherished
the name and title "father" most. Who could have
guessed this on the night he knocked on Bishop Myriel's
door?

> (Jean Valjean) said to Toussaint (the
> housekeeper), when she entered
> their service: "Mademoiselle (Co-
> sette) is the mistress o f the house."
> "And you, monsieur?" replied Touis-
> sant, astounded? "Me, I am much
> better than the master, I am the fa-
> ther." 8

Since my children are now grown and on their own, I
find it interesting that Jean Valjean's greatest challenge as
a parent came after Cosette's marriage. The old man felt
tossed in a storm of doubt about his new role in her life.
At a similar point, when my sense of "Father → father"
might have weakened, life surprised me with an invitation to probe more deeply into this mystical sense of
Me. Another phase of fatherhood appeared.

Several years ago, my faith community invited me to
lead a ministerial team charged with welcoming those
who come to us with the desire to learn who we are,
what we believe, value and hold sacred. Should they decide to join our community, we guide them along the
path of initiation into their newly chosen way of life.
This belated mission of spiritual parenting confirms the
movement that has taken place over the half-century of
my adult life.

Like Jean Valjean, I study signposts along the way of my journey—all different, yet pointing in one direction.

Who am I?

I am priestly *Father* ➜ adoptive *father* ➜ spiritual *father*.

I am Joseph.

That is Me.

Harvesting the Depth and Richness of My Life

Do I like my given name? How well does it fit what I perceive as the real Me?

_____
_____
_____
_____
_____
_____
_____
_____
_____
_____
_____

How much effort do I make to learn people's names when I meet them? Or to remember them, when I see them again?

_____
_____
_____
_____
_____
_____
_____
_____
_____
_____
_____
_____

Do I have some other "secret" name, known only to myself, one that fits me better than my given name(s)? What is it?

_____

_____

_____

_____

_____

_____

_____

_____

_____

_____

If I were to change my name right now, how would I choose to be called?

_____

_____

_____

_____

_____

_____

_____

_____

_____

_____

SHOCK AND AWE
OF PARENTHOOD

"Cosette"
by
Emile Bayard

from the original edition
of *Les Miserables*
(1862)

Introduction

Jean Valjean did not choose fatherhood. He had never loved or been loved for himself. The dying Fantine's love for her little Cosette anointed him the child's rescuer and guardian. Thus was set in motion a plan made in heaven. M. Madeleine, the disguised parolee, could only blame the late Charles-Francois-Bienvenu Myriel, Bishop of Digne for it. Although he could have denied this mother's plea, Jean Valjean's "phantom promise" vowed on the kindly cleric's doorstep rendered it unthinkable.

The crusty former convict's spirit erupted with feelings he had never before experienced. Alarmed at the responsibility thrust upon him, yet amazed at the peace and fulfillment his dawning love for Cosette evoked, he gazed upon the tableau of himself and the child. He became in Victor Hugo's words, "like a mother."

Like Jean Valjean, I arrived late at fatherhood and discovered within my untested heart an unaccustomed freshness and vitality. Although the "dad thing" had no place in my life's original blueprint, I am grateful that it grabbed hold and took possession of me.

A Heart Full of
Freshness (1)

*The dawn of the next day found Jean
Valjean again near the bed of Cosette.
He waited there, motionless, to see her
wake. Something new was entering his
soul. Jean Valjean had never loved anything. For twenty-five years he had been
alone in the world. He had never been a
father, lover, husband, or friend
 . . . . The heart of the old convict was
full of freshness.*

Cosette, Book Fourth, III:
Two Misfortunes Mingled
Make Happiness

ॐ

Reflection

Every new parent can identify with Victor Hugo's poignant description of Jean Valjean's first night with his child. We remain at our child's bedside "motionless," transformed forever as that "something new" enters our souls.

I have experienced two such nights. The first in 1987 at the Ramada Inn, San Salvador, El Salvador.[1] It was clear when my wife and I arrived at the orphanage that our almost four-year-old daughter had a fever. We drove directly to our attorney's pediatrician. Watching him draw blood from our little girl's arm, I discovered a universal truth of parenthood: watching your child suffer is greater than any personal pain.

Once back in our hotel room, we began a vigil similar to that of Hugo's protagonist. As yet, our child had not spoken to us, but we were not concerned about her silence. She needed to find out if she could entrust her life to these strangers. For our part, we dared not take our eyes off her. Someone might yet snatch her from us and our dream child might turn out to be just that.

I understand what Victor Hugo meant when he said of Jean Valjean that he had "never loved anything before." Not the literal truth, in my case. I had tasted love's sweet ecstasy. But I had never experienced anything like what I felt on my first night as a father.

Unfamiliar, primal feelings spread through me. I unearthed remnants of a prehistoric man guarding the mouth of his cave—protector of a vulnerable family member. I became human comfort personified at my ailing child's bedside. As temple priest I offered prayers and sacrifices to a distant yet mysteriously involved deity.

I also felt frightened and clueless, wishing we were back home and safe in California. And yes, like Jean Valjean, I overflowed with "freshness," awestruck by this new person forever laminated onto my life.

When our little Monica Carolina awoke the next morning, her temperature had fallen to normal. She spoke her first words to us: *"Mi dedo."*

I looked and, sure enough, under one of her (little) big toes I found a puffy blister that had gone unnoticed in the excitement and anxiety of the previous day.

At last, a problem I could do something about. I felt useful again.

Harvesting the Depth and Richness of My Life

In what way(s) do I identify with Jean Valjean's experience that "something new was entering his soul" when Cosette awoke in his presence for the first time?

How would I describe my first night with a new son or daughter?

If I am an adoptee, what is my earliest memory of my new parents? What stories and writings have they passed down to me about their feelings at the time of my adoption?

_____

_____

_____

_____

_____

_____

_____

_____

_____

_____

_____

_____

_____

How have I experienced the helplessness and anxiety of watching a child suffer?

_____

_____

_____

_____

_____

_____

_____

_____

_____

_____

_____

_____

A Heart Full
of Freshness (2)

The dawn of the next day found Jean Val-
jean again near the bed of Cosette. He
waited there, motionless, to see her wake.
Something new was entering his soul. Jean
Valjean had never loved anything. For
twenty-five years he had been alone in the
world. He had never been a father, lover,
husband, or friend . . . . The heart of the
old convict was full of freshness.

Cosette, Book Fourth, III:
Two Misfortunes Mingled
Make Happiness

&

Reflection

Jean Valjean experienced but one first morning with his adopted child. Life has blessed me with two such experiences. In 1988, a year after bringing our first daughter home, my wife and I traveled to Tegucigalpa, Honduras to arrange the adoption of another three-year-old girl. According to Honduran law at the time, adopting parents made two visits to the country. The first to inaugurate adoption proceedings in the Honduran court of minor children; the second, three months later, to finalize the adoption and obtain the visas required to bring her home to the United States.

Since the timing of the second journey coincided with the last days of preparation for Christmas, we decided that I should make the trip alone to bring our daughter home. It took until the day before our scheduled return for the local authorities to release Cristina into my custody. Finally, I could move her from the orphanage to the adoptive parents hostel. Our room contained a twin-sized bed for me and a crib for her. Because of the long travel day ahead (Tegucigalpa to Houston to San Francisco), I put her to bed early. Exhausted from the anxiety of the past few days, I needed a good night's sleep to reenergize. Such was my plan, at least.

Cristina refused to stay in the child's bed and insisted on being with me. Fatherly assurances that I would be right there when she awoke proved insufficient to allay her fears. She needed to be within arm's reach of her new dad. I relented, but she did not sleep. She clung to me through the night, kissing me repeatedly and telling me in her sweet little voice how much she loved me, despite the fact that she hardly knew me. How could she be sure that her new life in this place called America would be better than the safety and familiarity of the life she had left behind? I marveled at her trust and prayed to be worthy of it.

Cristina had to be hoping with all the desire of her little heart that I would turn out to be her knight in shining armor. In the unfair world she already knew too well, the odds were fifty-fifty that I had been sent as punishment for the tragic flaw that had caused her birth mother to abandon her and for leaving behind her country and the children and nuns who had been her only friends.

No wonder that I thought, when I read of Jean Valjean's first twenty-four hours as an adoptive father, "Monsieur Hugo, you got it right." For the second time in little over a year, "something new was entering (my) soul." This heart that had thought itself incapable of paternal love once again filled with freshness.

Harvesting the Depth and Richness of My Life

Before the birth or adoption of my first child, what
misgivings did I have about my readiness to assume
the responsibilities of parenthood?

_____
_____
_____
_____
_____
_____
_____
_____
_____
_____
_____

As a parent, what are my hopes and dreams for my children's future? What role do I see myself playing in their
adult lives?

_____
_____
_____
_____
_____
_____
_____
_____
_____
_____
_____

If I am an adoptive parent, what concerns did I have about my fitness to parent a child not my own flesh and blood?134

_____

_____

_____

_____

_____

_____

_____

_____

_____

_____

_____

_____

When I/we first made it known that I/we intended to adopt, what concerns did family and friends voice about the decision?
What outright negativity did I/we encounter?

_____

_____

_____

_____

_____

_____

_____

_____

_____

_____

_____

Learning the Dad Thing

*As to Jean Valjean, there was indeed
within him all manner of tenderness and
all manner of solicitude; but he was only
an old man who knew nothing at all.*

St. Denis, Book Third, IV:
Change of Grating

႙

Reflection

I was fifty-two at the time of our first adoption. I had spent all of my teens and most of my adult years in the all-male, celibate environment of seminary and priesthood. As a new father I felt as Jean Valjean did. I had no training for the most sacred task a man can assume: fathering a relinquished child. Especially, in my case, a little girl.

Responsible parenting is not easily learned on the job, but like most dads that is what I had to do. And so I began my new life in a state of utter cluelessness. I did have two invaluable human resources, one in the person of my teacher-wife (herself a first-time mom), the other within myself. I found my personal power source in a kind of love I had never before experienced. From the first moments of union with our new daughter—even as I fumbled with our bulky Pentax to capture the first mother-daughter embrace—a geyser erupted in my inexperienced heart. Through streaming tears I told myself, I don't know how to do this dad thing, but I'll learn.

And I did. Barely.

Each stage of childhood brought a new set of bewildering challenges. I had just grasped how to be a father to preschoolers, when my daughters—we had two by this time—had moved on to "big kids" school. Since Esther taught full-time and I worked a more flexible schedule, I drove the girls to school and picked them up. Every afternoon I arrived in the parking lot with a cluster of moms and waited for the children to rush from the building. We scanned the waves of identical uniforms searching for our own. Each of us shared a common desire to triumph in the successes of their day or lather balm on a fragile sense of Self, wounded by some catastrophic slight.

The cycle continued. Countless times during their growth from childhood into pre-teenage, then blooming adolescence, I felt the weary befuddlement of Jean Valjean. Like him, I was "only an old man" (at least aging) "who knew nothing at all."

What did I know of young womanhood? I had two sisters. One older and more an icon than an influence. An operatic prodigy, she had sung the lead role of Santuzza in *Cavalleria Rusticana* at age fourteen! My younger sister (by five years) was my pal, but in effect I had left her behind and out of mind when I entered the seminary as a high school freshman. My last "date" had been in seventh grade—a fast little number way ahead of me in boy-girl savvy. Nothing had "happened," to my disappointment and relief.

Fast forward, now, to the parent of two blossoming daughters. During their adolescence I felt like a man being dragged behind a two-horse team. The description that defined me—more internalized than spoken—was "clueless love." I call it in pidgin Greek *cluelesseon*: "a bewildered love, genuine and self-giving, residing primarily in parents, most often on the paternal side." You won't find it listed among the classical Greek terms: *filios* (friendship), *eros* (sexual attraction), *storge* (instinctual affinity), and *agape* (unconditional love). Were the ancients too proud—or embarrassed—to wedge this befuddled expression of love between *storge* and *agape*?

I still wince with pain when I recall my own parents' confusion and shock when, in my mid-forties, I announced my intention to leave the active priesthood . . . and had no idea what I would do with the second half of my life. From the perspective of lapsed time and my own experience as a parent, I can imagine my mom suffering sleepless nights in the weeks following that bombshell. I am sure she called on all her favorite saints. And they were many.

The patron "saint" of *cluelesseon*? Who else but Jean Valjean, who lived (if only in the mind of Victor Hugo) in and around Paris, France, during the early and mid-nineteenth century?

My daughters, though still quite young in my eyes, have grown to adulthood. I hold them close, while admiring them increasingly from afar as they venture farther out from our nest. I would like to say that I am less bewildered by these two women, but I confess to not understanding the thought and decision-making processes of their twenty-something generation. Being twice removed from it makes it all the harder.

Harvesting the Depth and Richness of My Life

When do I feel most "clueless" as a parent? How does this feeling of not understanding, or of being out of control, affect my parenting style and decisions?

_____
_____
_____
_____
_____
_____
_____
_____
_____
_____
_____

If I am an "older" parent, how do I identify with Jean Valjean's feeling of being "only an old man who knew nothing at all"?

_____
_____
_____
_____
_____
_____
_____
_____
_____
_____
_____

What do I find hopeful in the attitudes and behaviors of the "younger generation"? What disturbs me?

_____
_____
_____
_____
_____
_____
_____
_____
_____
_____
_____
_____

If I am a grandparent, when does this feeling of cluelessness come over me as I watch my children's children strive for adulthood? What is my proper role in my grandchild(ren)'s life/lives?

_____
_____
_____
_____
_____
_____
_____
_____
_____
_____
_____
_____
_____

The Primal Wound

Fate abruptly brought together, and wedded with its resistless power, these two shattered lives, dissimilar in years, but similar in sorrow. The one, indeed, was the complement of the other. The instinct of Cosette sought for a father, as the instinct of Jean Valjean sought for a child. To meet, was to find one another . . . . When their two souls saw each other, they recognized that they were mutually needed, and they closely embraced.

Cosette, Book Fourth, III:
Two Misfortunes Mingled
Make Happiness

&

Reflection

The above passage describes in poetic language what psychologist Nancy Newton Verrier calls the "primal wound"[1] of childhood abandonment. It also dredges up the memory of painful times in my own life.

Victor Hugo approaches the topic of emotional scars caused by abandonment with this keen insight: "Fate abruptly brought together . . . these two shattered lives, dissimilar in years, but similar in sorrow." Jean Valjean's "shatteredness" is central to the novel's theme of personal transformation—resurrection. To be revived, one must first experience emotional death. Jean Valjean's fractured Self had its origin in childhood poverty. It worsened when he assumed the daunting responsibility of providing for his sister and her children. His youth—and any hope of normal life—ended with his arrest and imprisonment for stealing a loaf of bread.

Cosette had suffered at the hands of the Thenardiers. Yet, her "shattering" drew its brackish water from a hidden well. In the perverse grip of her brokenness, Cosette found the loneliness and hardship of her life unbearable. Like every abandoned child, she would have concluded that something in her nature had to be so flawed that her own mother could not keep her.

In her Preface to the book, *The Primal Wound*, Verrier describes this as "a wound which is physical, emotional, psychological, and spiritual, a wound which causes pain so profound as to have been described as cellular by those adoptees who allowed themselves to go that deeply into the pain."[2]

I had a college professor who relished the expression, "You need to crack a few eggs to make an omelet." To me this reeked of self-bestowed superiority. That despised adage comes to mind now, but in a more positive context. Twice in my adult life, I have been "broken," only to remake myself into someone new, different and better.

Once Shattered

Three years after my ordination as a Roman Catholic priest, I awakened one morning in terror. I had never experienced such pervasive fright. I looked at my image in the mirror and said: "Who is this guy inside the black suit and white Roman collar? Who are you—really?"

I had no answer that made sense in the glare of my first-ever self-scrutiny. Without knowing who I was, I had made a lifetime commitment that imposed severe restrictions and potentially eternal penalties for infidelity! My psyche splintered with a soundless crash.

There followed fifteen years of self-examination and therapy-aided introspection about the triggering question of my identity. I picked up each shard of my Self. I studied it and either found its proper place in my rebuilt psyche or discarded it as a no longer authentic piece of the real Me. I never arrived at a definitive answer to my "Who am I?" investigation. I discovered, instead, that the search for Self is an unending, sometimes hazardous, journey.

If ever a shattered man existed in literature, it was Hugo's Jean Valjean. By the time he took responsibility for Cosette, he had erased all memory of the innocence and native goodness of his youth. He had committed countless evil deeds, but one in particular haunted him: the theft of forty sous from an urchin named Gervais. Committing this deed so soon after receiving pardon and freedom through the unconditional kindness of Bishop Myriel only added to Jean Valjean's self-disgust.

Long a stranger to close connection with other human beings, the feelings that flooded him at the sight of Fantine's child blind-sided him. Cosette's experience of this meeting mirrored his: "When their two souls saw each other, they recognized that they were mutually needed, and they closely embraced."

Twice Shattered

With a sense of grief and loss for those parts of my ministry that I loved but had to leave behind, I withdrew from active ministry in the church. For the first time in my life, I performed on a high wire without a safety net to catch me if I failed. Not having a job or any reliable roadmap to the future, I endured a second "shattering." Since I had survived my fifteen years earlier, I trusted God to help me forge a new life out of my self-chosen emptiness.

Whatever I endured during those two awful years before I met my wife meant nothing compared to the splintering my two daughters had experienced so early in their childhoods. I will not relate the details of their personal pre-adoption stories. That is their prerogative, should they ever choose to do so. My intent here is to affirm the experience of Jean Valjean and Cosette, as envisioned by Victor Hugo.

I needed the love of my daughters to make me whole, as much as they needed my love to restore them to wholeness after their abandonment. In parenthood, I discovered the treasured missing piece of fatherhood that clerical priesthood had denied me. When our souls met, we recognized that we were "mutually needed," and we "embraced."

I learned in time that love cannot heal the primal wound parental abandonment causes—even when that loss results from human desperation. For a long time I had refused to believe this. I told myself that love had the power to heal any emotional wound. The wise Nancy Newton Verrier convinced me otherwise. Adoptive parents must absorb, out of sheer proximity, the punishment intended for birth parents.

Such is the ebb and flow of life—being shattered, putting ourselves together, shattering again, then reassembling the pieces one by one.

Love, no matter how pure and unconditional, cannot allay the pain of the primal wound.

What love can do is keep the inner Self's assembly line moving forward towards wholeness.

Harvesting the Depth and Richness of My Life

In what way(s) have I experienced a "shattering" in my
life? What were my feelings at the time?
How close did I come to despair? How did I survive?

_____
_____
_____
_____
_____
_____
_____
_____
_____
_____
_____
_____

As a parent—adoptive or biological—how would I
describe the experience of needing my children as much
as they have needed me?

_____
_____
_____
_____
_____
_____
_____
_____
_____
_____
_____
_____

What experience do I have of a "primal wound," either in myself or in someone close to me? To what extent do I agree or disagree with Nancy Newton Verrier that there is no permanent cure for the effects of this kind of wound?

_____

_____

_____

_____

_____

_____

_____

_____

_____

_____

_____

_____

_____

_____

_____

_____

_____

_____

_____

_____

_____

_____

_____

_____

_____

Real-Life Fantines

*Jean Valjean bent down and kissed the
child's hand. Nine months before, he had
kissed the hand of the mother (Fantine),
who also had just fallen asleep.*

Cosette, Book Fourth, II:
A Nest for Owl and Wren

&

Reflection

That life is a mystery is no mystery. And love reigns atop the pyramid of unanswerable questions.

Jean Valjean's feelings for Fantine, nicknamed "The Blonde" in her innocent years, are a study in themselves. During his pre-bishop of Digne life, he had allowed himself only one emotion, rage. Spiritual and moral conversion had flung open the barred gates of his inner prison. Fantine's plight unleashed a host of first-time feelings that he would take to the grave unfathomed.

Like many needy young women, she had given her too generous heart to a man incapable of recognizing a treasure in human form. During the summer of 1817, he enjoyed, then discarded her in favor of a newer model. By then, Fantine had become pregnant and a poster girl for her class, *les miserables.*

Fantine entered Jean Valjean's life as a worker in his buckle factory where he treated and paid his employees better than other businessmen of his day. He did not know this young woman. Nor had he heard the rumors that Fantine had a child but no wedding band to justify her motherhood. Without his awareness or consent, the foreman in his factory had fired the young mother for the "sin" of needing money to feed her child.

Fantine lay ill and near death in the very hospital Jean Valjean himself had built when she came to his attention. He listened in horror to the wasted woman's tale of desperation. Out of love for her child, she had cut off her golden hair and sold it. When the price proved insufficient to finance Cosette's room and board, she had yanked the incisors from her mouth and sold them. Knowledge that this woman's fall into hopeless poverty had resulted from actions performed in his name filled Jean Valjean with remorse and pity. These feelings demanded reparation for the damage.

Getting to know Fantine during her illness, Jean Valjean fell in love with her (although Victor Hugo never employs this romantic language). Inspired by that love—tainted by the shame of complicity in her misery—Jean Valjean vowed to rescue Cosette and become her guardian. When Fantine died in his arms, he became the child's father.

In kissing his new daughter's hand he expressed his love for the only woman who had ever found permanent lodging in his heart. Embracing Fantine's child—now his own—and loving her with all his heart, served as daily homage to the mother.

Like Jean Valjean, I am an adoptive father. And like him my daughters' birth mothers often occupy my thoughts and prayers. I am beneficiary of treasures formed and nurtured like gold deep in the earth of their wombs. Imagine the agony that must have preceded the decisions, in one case to relinquish her child to strangers from another country, in the other to abandon her to the fickle providence of chance. Imagine their thoughts today when they wonder, gazing at the nighttime sky as they must at times, what became of their little girls.

Have you ever had a moment that generated feelings just the opposite of what you expected or would have scripted? The most topsy-turvy experience of my life took place at an umbrella-shaded table alongside the swimming pool at the San Salvador Ramada Inn in August, 1987. The Ramada was not the fanciest hotel in the capital, but it must have seemed luxurious to the twenty-something Rosa Elena, who had gifted us with her beautiful daughter. Had she been born into one of the country's ruling families, this woman might have been considered attractive. In her real-life circumstance as a roadside tortilla vendor with five children and an on-again-off-again day laborer partner, she appeared middle-aged, accelerating toward her final years.

From across the table, her juice drink sitting untouched, Rosa Elena—in true Fantine spirit—delivered an elegy for her shrinking motherhood. I paraphrase her Spanish: "I can't express the happiness I feel that you are taking my child to America. You can give her an education. She'll have opportunities I can't possibly give her." Any tears of anger, remorse, or envy that I had anticipated remained locked within her for release in private moments. Instead, a simple joy radiated from her bronzed face.

Esther and I wept at our unworthiness in the face of such unselfishness. After a year of personal and legal preparation, we had traveled to El Salvador as triumphant parents-to-be rejoicing in the fulfillment of our dream.

We came away from that encounter, not less exhilarated at the miracle that had transformed our lives, but a great deal humbler. Adoption has made me aware of the courage of *les miserables* and the undeserved suffering their status imposes. How do I contribute to the anguish that brought such joy to my life? Have we purchased our joy these past twenty-plus years with the poverty of this real-life Fantine?

In Honduras the following year, we did not have an opportunity for a face-to-face with our second daughter's birth mother. Instead, like Jean Valjean searching for the wronged urchin, Gervais, I felt her presence in every indigenous mother we encountered in the streets of Tegucigalpa, selling anything someone might buy for a few lempiras.

These two women arise in my consciousness when I read that Jean Valjean remembered Fantine as he kissed Cosette's hand. As a First World citizen, gratitude and remorse pull me in opposite directions. I am grateful to my daughters' birth mothers for giving them life. I am indebted to them for their generosity—regardless of the motivation that drove it. I received each child as a miracle of destiny. At the same time, I grieve that their mothers' sacrifices occurred on my watch as a citizen of planet Earth.

At that poolside table in 1987, I swore a vow more sacred than any I had given to the Church as a priest. I promised Rosa Elena that I would do everything in my power to fulfill her dream for this one-too-many child. A year later I repeated that promise by proxy in the absence of a flesh-and-blood mother. I have done my best to be faithful to my commitment. If God would let these moms see their raggedy little girls all grown, loving, intelligent, and dedicated to making a difference in our world, they would glow with maternal pride.

Harvesting the Depth and Richness of My Life

What gifts do I enjoy in my life that were or might have been purchased by the sufferings of other less fortunate men and women—perhaps even children?

_____
_____
_____
_____
_____
_____
_____
_____
_____
_____
_____

What circumstances would have to exist for me to part with one of my children?

_____
_____
_____
_____
_____
_____
_____
_____
_____
_____
_____

When have I had an experience in which my emotions were quite the opposite of what I would have expected in that situation?

_____
_____
_____
_____
_____
_____
_____
_____
_____
_____
_____

If I am an adoptive parent, what feelings do I have for my child(ren)'s birth parents?

_____
_____
_____
_____
_____
_____
_____
_____
_____
_____
_____

A Gift in the Present Tense

*Nature had placed a wide chasm—fifty years'
interval of age—between Jean Valjean and
Cosette. This chasm fate filled up. Fate
abruptly brought together, and wedded with its
resistless power, these two shattered lives, dissimilar in years, but similar in sorrow. The
one, indeed, was the complement of the other.
The instinct of Cosette sought for a father, as
the instinct of Jean Valjean sought for a child.
To meet, was to find one another. . . .
When their two souls saw each other, they recognized that they were mutually needed, and
they closely embraced.*

Cosette, Book Fourth, III:
Two Misfortunes Mingled
Make Happiness

࿇

Reflection

I am struck by the coincidence that both Jean Valjean and I were half-a-century older than our adopted children. He was fifty-eight, Cosette eight; I fifty-two, Monica three. A year later Cristina, also three, came into our lives. From the beginning of our time together, my advanced age has been an influencing factor in our lives. When, in the rejuvenation of new parenthood, I forgot my chronological age, people in playgrounds and restaurants reminded me with, "You have the cutest grandchildren."

During our daughters' growing up years I was often the oldest parent in the back-to-school night classroom, the oldest jock-dad in the bleachers at basketball and softball games. In self-defense I developed a list of advantages in being a generation older than other kids' parents:

1. By the time of our adoptions, I had a good idea of my selfhood and didn't need to search for it while making parenting decisions. My road to adult self-knowledge had been a long and not always pleasant one. As in every other major aspect of my life I got a late start. In fact, I mark my thirtieth year as the starting point. Having tasted the dawn of maturity, I made its attainment my top priority for the next two decades.

2. The proverbial "school of hard knocks," combined with my formal education, had brought me far along the path of understanding how the major pieces of my life fit together: family, career, money, personal values (in no way a complete list).

3. I had survived my personal midlife angst in the preceding decade, before marrying and having children.

Having made a commitment to dedicate my life to service of the Roman Catholic Church as a priest, I had to deal with the uncomfortable possibility of being called to serve God in some other way. I hadn't a clue what that meant, but leapt into the void nonetheless. In that great ocean of the unknown, I found a level of fulfillment I had never dreamed possible. By the time of our adoptions, I had less chance of chasing after some youth-preserving fantasy.

4. I could answer my children's life questions with some wisdom about the highest potential of human nature and the realities of human weakness—and forgiveness. Questions such as: Why did my parents abandon me? Why do some friends betray me? Why do I look different from everyone else in this family? Why do I feel like I don't "belong."

To our daughters' credit, they have never expressed or implied by their attitudes or actions that they felt cheated by having an older father. From the beginning they have appreciated the anchor such a parent can provide when life's storms threaten.

Growing from their teens into college-age adults, they witnessed peers' families fragment because their parents had not yet discovered their own true selves—or they discovered their true identities too late, after marrying and having children. These parents had to work through their own identity issues at a time when their growing children needed the safe harbor of wisdom and mature modeling.

Having experienced firsthand the effects of adult misguidance on some of their close friends, our daughters have expressed in Father's Day, Mother's Day and birthday cards an appreciation for our parenting style.

I cannot deny the shadowy downside to being an older parent. It worried Jean Valjean that he might not live to see Cosette into adulthood and a solid marriage— a young woman's primary social salvation in the nineteenth century. I, too, think about this, but within a twenty-first century context. I am grateful that I have accompanied my daughters into their early adulthood and seen them settle into life as educated, independent women. Apart from the creative imagination of the author of his story, Jean Valjean had no control over his life span. Similarly, my future is in the hands of my Author.

Victor Hugo allowed his protagonist to follow Cosette as far as marriage to a man who adored her— almost as much as her father did. Grandchildren? Those he would have to shower with doting attention from the afterlife in which he believed.

I prefer not to think too much about how my father story will end. Being my children's dad is a daily gift. It lives in the present tense.

Harvesting the Depth and Richness of My Life

If I am two generations removed from my children's age, in what ways does this disturb me or cause feelings of insecurity?

_____

_____

_____

_____

_____

_____

_____

_____

_____

_____

What do I know about parenting now that I wish I had known when my children were little? When they were in elementary and middle school? High school?

_____

_____

_____

_____

_____

_____

_____

_____

_____

_____

_____

What is my dream as a parent for my children's future? What role do I see myself playing in their adult lives?

_____

_____

_____

_____

_____

_____

_____

_____

_____

_____

If I am one of those "older" parents, what do I see as the advantages and disadvantages of the age difference between myself and my child(ren)?

_____

_____

_____

_____

_____

_____

_____

_____

_____

_____

Like a Mother

(Jean Valjean) would approach the bed where (Cosette) slept, and would tremble there with delight; he felt inward yearnings, like a mother, and knew not what they were; for it is something very incomprehensible and very sweet, this grand and strange emotion of the heart in its first love.

Cosette, Book Fourth, III:
Two Misfortunes Mingled
Make Happiness

☙

Reflection

Recalling my first year as parent, I identify with this "grand and strange emotion of the heart" experienced by the rough-hewn, formerly loveless, friendless Jean Valjean.

For a nineteen-year period beginning with his early adulthood, Jean Valjean had known only the brutality of prison. Those lost years had deprived him of the experiences of other young men—honest work, courtship, marriage, fatherhood. At the dawn of adulthood, the tree pruner with a low-wage income had assumed responsibility for his sister and her fatherless children. Despite his good intentions, he had not been able to earn enough to provide for that first family. Years later, the paroled convict could not recall the names or faces of those nieces and nephews for whom he had committed that innocent crime. Nor did he know what had become of them.

At the time he received Cosette into his care, Jean Valjean was no longer the naïve youth. Since his encounter with Bishop Myriel, he had retreated into the shadows, hiding behind one alias after another. At night he slept but did not rest. Each morning he awoke to dread of discovery.

These are hardly qualifications for adoption home-study approval. But Jean Valjean had promised to redeem Cosette. And more—to raise the child himself.

Financially secure, thanks to the bishop's endowment and his own successful manufacturing enterprise, Jean Valjean possessed the means to support Cosette for life. What he lacked—or thought he did—was an understanding of what it meant to be a father. What did he know of a little girl's need for nourishment, companionship, and education?

Jean Valjean did what I had done long before reading Hugo's novel. He let Cosette teach him the ways of parental love. Like all involved new fathers, he discovered that a loving heart is not the reserve of mothers. Dads, too, approach a new child's bed and "tremble there with delight." We experience with Jean Valjean "inward yearnings, like a mother."

Harvesting the Depth and Richness of My Life

How would I describe the emotions that stir in me when I think about my responsibility for my child(ren)'s safety and care?

_____

_____

_____

_____

_____

_____

_____

_____

_____

_____

_____

To what extent do I identify with Jean Valjean's awakening tenderness to his newly adopted child?

_____

_____

_____

_____

_____

_____

_____

_____

_____

_____

_____

If I am a father, in what ways am I aware of loving
my child differently from my wife or parenting partner?

_____
_____
_____
_____
_____
_____
_____
_____
_____
_____
_____
_____
_____
_____

As a mother, how does my style of parenting differ from
that of my husband or parenting partner?

_____
_____
_____
_____
_____
_____
_____
_____
_____
_____
_____
_____
_____

THE POWER OF STORY

Introduction

Stories. What would a family be without this medium for symbolic truth telling? As a novelist I sometimes find myself in conversation defending the proposition that fiction is a secure depository of truth.

Question: "If your story is not factual, how can you say it's true?"

Author: "The story is 'made up,' but I intend to convey the reality of some aspect of life. My characters may be inventions, but there is an underlying genuineness in the way they relate to each other, in their virtues and vices, their solutions to real-world problems."

As a lay minister in a large parish, I might say it like this: "The Bible is a library. One of its areas is the Fiction section, where we find stories that may not be historical but have survived for millennia because of some truth that still makes sense and speaks to our lives today."

My storytelling years as a dad predated my professional fiction writing career. Although I love reading and writing novels, I do miss the oral tradition of my daughters' childhood. Their beds were the campfires around which we stirred each others' imaginations, made each other laugh, and spoke the truth about life and love.

Healing Stories

To teach Cosette to read, and to watch her
playing, was nearly all Jean Valjean's life.
And then, he would talk about her mother.

Cosette, Book Fourth, III:
Two Misfortunes Mingled
Make Happiness

಄

Reflection

In the aftermath of September 11, 2001, surviving parents and spouses shared tales of dedication and heroism, extolling those who had lost their lives in the tragedies of that day.

A law written upon the human heart compels us to let our sons and daughters know that the loss they suffered did not result from a decision to abandon. That same heart-law imposes a corresponding obligation to impart that oral history with delicate honesty and, if need be, judicious selectivity. Obedient to this statute, Jean Valjean spoke to Cosette about her mother. The revelations must have included Fantine's dying wish to provide for her daughter herself, not by proxy. Her exhausted body failed to match her strength of will.

The Storyteller's Need

Buried within the complexity of the human heart lies another, often hidden, need—that of the surviving parent. In Jean Valjean's case, preserving these stories kept Fantine alive to him, in the way it does for any spouse whose grief preserves the best of a loving relationship.

For some survivors, Jean Valjean being one, that need is lifelong. No subsequent love can match the first—or replace it. Other widows and widowers, whose love flamed with equal passion and whose loss seared no less, find comfort in new relationships that are different but satisfying and no less committed.

I have not suffered the loss of my spouse and pray to be spared that common marital reality. The closest I have come to Jean Valjean's kind of telling is what I have communicated to my daughters about my own deceased mother, their grandmother. I've told them about this beautiful, generous and loving woman. Had she known them, she would have received them into her heart with total and forever love. She would have relished hugging them close to her welcoming body. And filled their bellies with steaming bowls of pasta and slices of Sicilian-style pizza.

Jean Valjean must have shared with Cosette memories similar to these, though his entire experience of Fantine was that of an ill and emaciated woman. His image of the beauty of her youth lacked eyewitness verification. With these tales, he presented her to Cosette in a resurrected body that matched her perfect spirit.

Integration of Needs

In revealing these intimate father-daughter moments, Victor Hugo provides yet another layer of insight into the complexity of the human spirit. In telling Cosette about her mother, the elderly Jean Valjean offered her a priceless gift, but not to her alone. Within the most generous gift giving resides a trace of self-service.

So it is with the stories a parent like Jean Valjean tells to a child who has lost a mommy or daddy. Little by little, the telling and retelling diminish the pain of loss and refill the depleted spirit.

Regardless of whose need stories of life and death satisfy, there is power in the sharing.

Harvesting the Depth and Richness of My Life

How do I talk to children about beloved family
members they never had an opportunity to know?

_____

_____

_____

_____

_____

_____

_____

_____

_____

_____

_____

_____

_____

What do I say to children about beloved family
members they knew—and lost?

_____

_____

_____

_____

_____

_____

_____

_____

_____

_____

_____

_____

Whose need am I fulfilling when I relate to my
children or other people stories about my parent(s)
whom I have lost in death?

Do I sometimes choose not to mention my deceased
loved ones' imperfections? If so, why?

Bedtime Stories

*When he saw Cosette, when he had
taken her, carried her away, and rescued her, he felt his heart moved. All
that he had of feeling and affection was
aroused and vehemently attracted
towards this child. He would approach
the bed where she slept, and would
tremble there with delight; he felt
inward yearnings, like a mother, and
knew not what they were; for it is something very incomprehensible and very
sweet, this grand and strange emotion
of the heart in its first love.*

Cosette, Book Fourth, III:
Two Misfortunes Mingled
Make Happiness

&

Reflection

There is a clumsy gentleness in the fifty-something Jean Valjean's early experience of parenthood. Observing Cosette in peaceful sleep, his once unfeeling heart soared in contemplation of the sacred responsibility he had assumed.

Some of my happiest memories as a dad are those of getting my little girls ready and settled for the night. As in most families, our bedtime routine progressed through established phases beginning with baths and the donning of storybook character nightclothes. The ceremony continued with "tucking in," which wasn't complete until I had stretched the bedspreads all the way to their chins. Then, I would look about in puzzlement.

"Are there any little girls in here?" I followed the script to the letter.

Silence.

"Guess not. I'll just wait till they get here"—at which I moved to one of the beds and sat on top of a little body. Jumping in mock fright, I'd gasp, "What's that?"

Giggles and screams rang throughout the kids' stuffed animal kingdom.

I loved—and still miss—our story times. Rarely did we read from a book, although *Good Night Moon* remained an oft-recycled favorite. The nightly ritual called for me to continue with: "What kind of story do you want tonight?" Their prompts challenged my imagination and improvisational skills, but I soon discovered literary resources concealed beneath my decades of crusty adult living. I cherished this challenge to invent a cast of characters featuring two lovely princesses (whose names happened to be the same as my daughters').

Handsome knights and lords with hearts brave and true sprang to life. In our fantasy world, good guys won; bad guys had no chance. The princesses always got their men.

The Short family held a high place among my personal favorite tales. They went for short walks and stayed out for only a short time. In fact everything they said, did or thought was . . . short. Since my daughters, even in adulthood, have grown to barely five feet, this story took on prophetic proportions in family lore.

Our bedtime finale consisted of a prayer in Spanish, taught to our younger daughter by the nuns at her Tegucigalpa orphanage. *"O Dios, amante de la vida, que visteis los pajaros del cielo . . . ."*[1]

Before turning out the lights, I had instructions to "debug" the room of spiders and banish any closeted monsters. Only with my solemn assurance of their safety did my daughters grant permission to return to my grown-up world.

Leaving the bedroom door open just a crack, I left them to dream the dreams of little girls whose first three years of life were known to them alone. For all my ability to chase creepy-crawlies from under their beds and goblins from their closet, I felt powerless to exorcise imprinted memories of rejection and the night terrors of abandonment.

Jean Valjean vowed to erase all the suffering Cosette's had endured at the hands of the Thenardiers. I prayed for healing of my daughters' conscious and subconscious recollections. I offered my love as a balm to cover wounds I knew would never close. Failing a cure, I hoped my goofy antics and fanciful stories at the end of their day would at least anesthetize the hurt.

Harvesting the Depth and Richness of My Life

What is my fondest memory of my own or my child(ren)'s bedtime rituals?

_____
_____
_____
_____
_____
_____
_____
_____
_____
_____
_____

If my children are beyond "bedtime story" age, what do I miss most about those years of their lives?

_____
_____
_____
_____
_____
_____
_____
_____
_____
_____
_____

What were my childhood fears, if any, when the lights went out?

_____

_____

_____

_____

_____

_____

_____

_____

_____

_____

_____

_____

_____

What was my own favorite bedtime story?
What in particular about this story touched my heart?

_____

_____

_____

_____

_____

_____

_____

_____

_____

_____

_____

_____

What made-up stories do/did I tell my children? If there is/was a recurring theme, what is/was it?

Lost Angels

To teach Cosette to read, and to watch her playing, was nearly all Jean Valjean's life. And then, he would talk about her mother.

Cosette, Book Fourth, III:
Two Misfortunes Mingled
Make Happiness

‽

Reflection

Jean Valjean must have discovered soon after taking Fantine's child into his care that not even his heartfelt attachment to the little girl could love away her loss. Nor could he erase Cosette's earliest memories of rejection and humiliation, suffered at the hands of the Thenardiers.

Being a good father, Jean Valjean spoke often to Cosette of the mother she had never known. This elderly guardian, who knew nothing of modern parenting techniques, followed the counsel of his love for both mother and daughter. Wounded and scarred himself and grieving the woman he loved, he intuited that Cosette, too, suffered from a "primal wound" that festered at the core of their shared abandonment.

Jean Valjean possessed a special antidote with which he revived Cosette's numbed spirit—the gift of healing stories. He recounted her mother's eternal love and her dying wish to have her child at her side, as in former, better times. Jean Valjean held back from Cosette the truth that, in her mother's quest to achieve that reunion, she had sold her golden hair and perfect teeth. And, with nothing left of commercial value, her body, too. In a final act of desperation, Fantine had entrusted her child to M. Madeleine, the very man she had once blamed for her loss of employment.[1]

Piece by piece and in carefully edited versions of that history, Jean Valjean restored all that was healable in Cosette's spirit, leaving the rest to the Ultimate Healer of Souls.

Throughout my daughters' childhoods, I used stories and parables to shed light on the meaning of their lives.

Some dealt with actual events in our family life; others combined fact and fiction. All the stories were true in their own way and intended to heal wounds I had not inflicted and could not cure.

One bedtime story in particular drew frequent requests: "Daddy, tell us about our angels!"

"The ones who made a terrible mistake?" I knew exactly which parable they meant.

"Yes, that one."

After getting them settled, I began the familiar story:

> When it was time for you to be born, God gave each of you an angel who had instructions to deliver you directly to Mom and me here in California. But something went wrong. Your angels forgot the directions, or something. Anyway, they got lost. Instead of delivering you to us, they brought one of you to El Salvador, the other to Honduras to other mothers and fathers who gave birth to you and took care of you the best they could. Somehow—don't ask me to explain it—these good people sensed that something wasn't quite right. They had received misplaced children. And so, they began to search for your true parents.
>
> Meanwhile, back in California, Mom and I were saying to each other: "What could have happened to those girls?" We waited some more until we decided, "We'd better

go looking for them." It took a long time, but first we found Monica in El Salvador! Then we found Cristina next door in Honduras. Now at last, we're all together, just the way God planned it from the beginning.

In answer to our daughters' concern for what might have become of those errant angels, the best I could offer was: "I suppose God assigned them to new jobs that didn't require delivering children to families."

Harvesting the Depth and Richness of My Life

In what sense were bedtime stories healing for me
when I was a child?

_____

_____

_____

_____

_____

_____

_____

_____

_____

_____

If I have small children now, what are their favorite
stories? In what way might these tales possess some
healing qualities for them?

_____

_____

_____

_____

_____

_____

_____

_____

_____

_____

What role do "healing stories" play in my personal faith tradition (Bible, Koran, Book of Mormon, etc.)?

_____

_____

_____

_____

_____

_____

_____

_____

_____

_____

_____

_____

As an adult, what movies, plays, or books have affected me in a way that I might call healing for my grown-up spirit?

_____

_____

_____

_____

_____

_____

_____

_____

_____

_____

_____

_____

A FATHER'S FAREWELL:

THE LAST WORDS
OF
JEAN VALJEAN

*Come closer, come closer, both of you. I love
you dearly. Oh! It is good to die so!*

Jean Valjean, Book Ninth, V:
Night Behind Which is Dawn

જી

Introduction

On the day of Cosette's marriage to Marius Pontmercy,[1] Ultimus Fauchelevent accompanied the bride
and groom to the civil registry, then to the church. In all
respects he behaved as the proud father releasing his
daughter safely into the hands of a man of means and
social status. As the reception began, the bride's father
begged their leave to return home on the pretense of
pain in his bandaged arm.

In fact, no such injury existed. Fauchelevent had
plotted in detail this withdrawal from his daughter's
life. He had his reasons, as he always did, and they knit
together into a blanket of painful wisdom. In confidence,
Fauchelevent had revealed to his son-in-law everything
about his former life and precarious legal status—even
his true name.

> I have one thing to tell you. I am
> an old convict.[2] My name is not
> Fauchelevent, my name is Jean Val-
> jean. I am nothing to Cosette . . . .
> She was an orphan. Without father
> or mother. She had need of me.
> That is why I began to love her.[3]

At the end of this confession he sought, as Catholics do, a penance as a sign of true repentance.

> "Now that you know, do you think, monsieur, you who are the master, that I ought not to see Cosette again?"
> "I think that would be best," answered Marius coldly.
> "I shall not see her again," murmured Jean Valjean.
> "You will come every evening," said Marius, "and Cosette will expect you."
> "You are kind, monsieur," said Jean Valjean.
> Marius bowed to Jean Valjean, happiness conducted despair to the door, and these two men separated.[4]

Jean Valjean continued to visit Cosette each evening, but not in the part of the house to which she had invited him as an honored family member. They met in the servants' area, in a room off the kitchen. Though unhappy with this arrangement, Cosette had no choice but to acquiesce or suffer the unthinkable alternative. In time, Jean Valjean's visits ceased altogether.

Hugo tells us:

> "At heart, (Cosette) really loved him whom she had so long called father. But she loved her husband still more."[5]

Reenter the former innkeeper, M. Thenardier. Aiming to extort money from Marius, the lone survivor of the battle at the barricades, Thenardier unwittingly dropped the final piece into the puzzle of this conflicted husband's life. Marius learned that the same father-in-law he now shunned was the one who had dragged him to safety through the sewers of Paris.

Desperate to apologize for his ill-treatment of Jean Valjean, Marius took Cosette and rushed to Rue de l'Homme Arme, Number 7.

They found Jean Valjean on his deathbed, having just written his daughter a farewell letter. It was summer, 1833, the year of her marriage.

Memories

To Me They are Gold

To (Cosette) I bequeath the two candle-sticks . . . they are silver; but to me they are gold. They are diamond; they change the candles which are put into them, into consecrated tapers.

Jean Valjean, Book Ninth, V:
Night Behind Which is Dawn

℘

Reflection

The candlesticks! Like bookends they stand at the beginning, not of Jean Valjean's chronological existence, but his real life. That life began the night the paroled convict stole everything of value from Bishop Myriel except these two treasures—and only because he had no way to conceal them. Those seminal gifts are close at hand in the hour of Jean Valjean's death.

This passage sends me searching for the bookends of my life . . . those pieces and parts of myself that I claim as treasures beyond price, the ordinary transformed into gold, diamonds.

Like Jean Valjean, I observe my life in two parts— not separate, yet distinct. Also like him, my dividing point occurred at early middle age.

As a young man I felt called to service in the church. During the 1940s and 50s, Catholics narrowly defined the concept of ministry within priesthood and a vowed religious life.

By midlife I had come to a painful spirit-place where I had to choose between continued ministry within the ranks of official clergy and a spiritual instinct to follow a path without roadmap or clear destination. At risk was the loss of ministry as I had known and loved it.

Three decades later, I find myself emotionally and spiritually richer, more committed than ever to my core beliefs, and once again engaged in the kind of ministry that had captured my imagination as an idealistic teen and twenty year old. And so, I expose the bookends of my life—my silver candlesticks.

Unwilling to send the ungrateful, undeserving beggar back to prison, Bishop Myriel parted with the last pieces

of his family heirlooms as definitive proof of his love—
God's love. This gift became the currency of a sacred,
but to Jean Valjean unholy, bargain that transferred
ownership of his life. "I am purchasing your soul," the
bishop had told him, "and I withdraw it from the spirit
of perversity, and I give it to God Almighty."[1] The beneficiary accepted the silver but rejected the implicit
promise of conversion.[2]

Neither in good times nor in bad did Jean Valjean
display his silver candlesticks. Periodically in need of
funds, he disappeared for a day or two, leaving Cosette
in the care of a trusted housekeeper. His travel took him
to that secret place where he had buried his fortune in
the earth. There, he unwrapped the candlesticks and
looked at them. They reminded him of the original gift,
his "phantom" promise, and the grace of his conversion.[3]

As the end of his life drew near, Jean Valjean removed his fortune from its hiding place for the last time.
The cash, 600,000 francs in all, became the old recluse's
wedding gift to his daughter and her husband. Only the
candlesticks remained in his possession—and 500 francs
willed to the poor.

With his dying words, Jean Valjean revealed to
Cosette what these precious light bearers meant to him:
"They are silver; but to me they are gold. They are diamond." With his next breath, Jean Valjean displayed an
uncommon depth of spiritual insight. After chronicling
the candlesticks' past and illuminating their current value
to him, he reaffirmed their power to affect future behavior.

. . . they change the candles which
are put into them, into consecrated tapers.

With these words, Victor Hugo demonstrated his be-
lief in the transformative power of material creation, in
this case silver, a mineral of the earth. The candlesticks
turned the tapers they bore into sacred lights. In the
course of the novel, we witness Jean Valjean's conversion from paroled thief to a model of integrity. What
originating spark set his life-change ablaze? An obscure
country bishop's single act of forgiveness and generosity.

No conversion is once-forever, not even the most
dramatic. The light of each dawn calls us to renewed
commitment. Each "retreat" to Jean Valjean's buried
treasure, each re-viewing of those candlesticks invited a
"yes" to the change that had taken place in him.

And what of the candlesticks' future effectiveness?
The dying man warned his daughter that in receiving
them, she must accept their spiritual power. The gift that
changed his life ordained Cosette to be for others, as he
was, a taper blessed and consecrated.

What sacred treasures will I pass to my Cosettes
when my time comes? Not much in worldly wealth
awaits them. My bequest can only consist of the twin
candlesticks that have endured exposure, burial, and resurrection over the course of my life. On the left, the
example of a life lived in light and shadow, but with ultimate hope and faith. On the right, an all-too-timid but
genuine commitment to making a difference in the world
through service.

It seems so little.

I pray it's enough.

Harvesting the Depth and Richness of My Life

What discernible "bookends" do I recognize in my life?
How do they define my life in terms of meaning,
purpose, history, etc.?

_____
_____
_____
_____
_____
_____
_____
_____
_____
_____
_____
_____

Who has been most the influential person in my life,
guiding me to become the man or woman I am today?

_____
_____
_____
_____
_____
_____
_____
_____
_____
_____
_____
_____

Who has played the catalytic role of Bishop Myriel in my life? What life-altering treasure(s) have I received from this person?

_____
_____
_____
_____
_____
_____
_____
_____
_____
_____

What core values do I hope to pass on to my children and loved ones when I reach the end of my life? How congruent is my present life with this goal?

_____
_____
_____
_____
_____
_____
_____
_____
_____
_____

Is He Pleased With Me?

I don't know whether he who gave (the candlesticks) to me is satisfied with me in heaven. I have done what I could.

Jean Valjean, Book Ninth, V:
Night Behind Which is Dawn

℘

Refection

On his deathbed, Jean Valjean experienced a moment of doubt that touches a sensitive—even painful—place in me and, I suspect, in the universal human spirit.

Have I done enough?

Are those who matter most to me, living or deceased, pleased with my life?

Jean Valjean hoped Bishop Myriel would look favorably upon his life's work and say, "That silver dinnerware and those candlesticks, now that was a good investment."

Entrapped by his phantom promise, Victor Hugo's once-bitter, self-indulgent outcast had seized the reins of love and soared to the heights as a devoted father and a man dedicated to assisting those in need. With time running out for further heroism, Jean Valjean wondered what grade might appear on his final report card. Had he indeed compounded the investment that launched his transformation from a life of moral darkness to a new existence in the light of resurrection?[1]

In the end, Jean Valjean relied on the only answer any of us can offer in summation of our lives: "I have done what I could."[2]

His deathbed doubt touches a musty place in my heart that I have not explored for nearly thirty years. I had lived long into adulthood with a tainted desire to prove to my parents that their middle child was just as good—if not better (and I tried so hard to be better)—than their firstborn and their baby. At the gates of midlife I mustered the courage to search out and give voice to my own mind and heart.

I have forgotten many things, but I will never forget sitting alone with my parents in their tiny family kitchen. The walls still carried the aroma of thousands of meals cooked from scratch, the result of Mom's daily multiplication of loaves and fishes. I had driven nearly four hundred miles to be with them and arrived late in the evening. We sat around the Formica-topped table a dozen feet from my old bedroom (barely a pantry on the main route from the kitchen to the only bathroom). A narrow cot on which I slept even then, when staying overnight, filled the space between the walls.

Surrounded by reminders of my docile youth, I broke the news that I had made a life-changing decision—one I had not prepared them for. We shed tears and exchanged some hurtful words.

At the end, my father looked at me and asked—as if I knew the answer—"What will become of us now?" How could I not have known that my parents had entwined their self-image with my status as a priest?

On my deathbed, will I wonder if I have pleased them? Who knows what shadows and doubts my end time will evoke?

Like Jean Valjean, I have done what I could.

Harvesting the Depth and Richness of My Life

Who, if anyone—living or dead—am I still trying to
please with my life?

Putting myself in Jean Valjean's deathbed scene, whom
might I look to on the "other side," wondering if I have
lived up to their hopes and dreams for me?
What do I need to say to my Bishop Myriel?

Secret Love

Jean Valjean to Cosette:
"The time has come for me to tell you the name of your mother. Her name was Fantine. Remember that name: Fantine. Fall on your knees whenever you pronounce it. She suffered much. And loved you much. Her measure of unhappiness was as full as your happiness (as Marius's wife)."

Jean Valjean, Book Ninth, V:
Night Behind Which is Dawn

಄

Reflection

Reading this deathbed passage, I react with a puzzled: "Jean Valjean never told Cosette her mother's name?" What else had he kept from her? That her mother had earned her threadbare living as a prostitute? That she had sold body parts to pay the blood-sucking Thenardiers for her daughter's room and board?

Granting Jean Valjean the parenting standards of his time and culture, I am aware of my own struggle with similar issues. Have I told my daughters everything I know about their pre-Garrotto lives? Not the whole story, but I will hold back nothing if they ask.

I wonder if Jean Valjean also concealed the fact that in Fantine he had found the secret and only love of his life—his spirit spouse and soul mate.

> . . . it might be said that, separated from everything by the walls of (Fantine's) tomb, Jean Valjean was the husband bereaved, as Cosette was the orphan.[1]

Victor Hugo never tells his readers that Jean Valjean "fell in love" with Cosette's dying mother. Rather, he shows us a man, whose every kind deed, every healing word to this unfortunate young woman evidenced a deepening bond. This love had its unpromising origin in guilt and remorse for his perceived complicity in Fantine's financial dilemma and suffering. As he witnessed the beauty—sanctity, even—of this scarred woman's soul, Jean Valjean's feelings segued into the uncharted terrain of total, unending devotion.

Love? What did he know of human love? He had no prior experience against which to measure what had taken place at the opaque core of his heart. Sexual desire? No woman had ever befriended him, drawn him into the welcoming inner chambers of her life. As mayor of Montreuil-sur-Mer, he had gained admirers for heroism, entrepreneurism and philanthropy, but only the bishop had treated him as a unique and worthy human being.

The parallel isn't precise but I, too, once had a secret love that caused my heart to race ahead of understanding. I began this story in an earlier Reflection, "The Violence of Thought." Now, it seems appropriate to share the rest.

Apart from a stream of youthful infatuations, my first experience of adult love sneaked up on me, catching body and spirit unawares. It began with a Christmas card. The writer and I had worked together several years earlier. We had "hit if off," until she moved away to teach in another part of the state. I did not acknowledge the card, but neither did I discard it. It remained on my desk until the following Easter, when I must have been, like Jean Valjean, ripe for intimacy without consciously seeking or desiring it.

I responded to my friend's Christmas message. This delayed exchange launched a long-distance relationship, linked mostly—in those pre-e-mail and instant messaging days—by snail-mailed audio tapes. Separation assured fidelity to my celibate commitment and her religious vows, while fostering intimacy. In the months that followed, my days spiked like heartbeats on an electrocardiogram whenever a small package brought me her sweet and gentle voice.

Infrequently, we managed a day together, which heightened the intensity of our attachment. I recall a sunbathed drive from Orange County to Santa Barbara. Oh, and that Fourth of July ferry ride to the beach on Angel Island, snuggling later that evening under a blanket of fog at a drive-in theater somewhere in San Francisco.

Over the next two years our verbal and emotional intimacies satisfied a need I had not been aware of. Like children playing a game of make-believe, we had stepped through the back of a wardrobe into a safe and glorious way of being.

In the end, one heart lay exposed and broken—mine. Inexperience in the ways of adult relationships had blinded me to signs that we had exceeded our allotted time. She arrived at this truth before I did and abruptly terminated our magical fantasy. In the real world of adult communication, her "I can't do this anymore," meant, "We can't."

Had I truly been in love? Or had I experienced a more intense infatuation than others my heart had entertained? If not the real thing, I cherish that relationship as a precursor, prepping me for a new way of experiencing life.

Kneeling beside Fantine's deathbed, Jean Valjean had committed himself to her as much as any husband had to his wife. His beloved's death unleashed in him all the devastation and emptiness of widowhood. He had lost a spouse without acknowledging one had existed. And the child Cosette who had yet to enter his life? No wonder he took her to himself as "father," despite his lack of preparation for this most sacred of male roles.

The shadowy nature of Jean Valjean's existence through the subsequent years allowed him no safe outlet for his grief. In whom could he confide what Fantine had meant to him? Whatever Victor Hugo's protagonist told Cosette about her mother through the years of her growing up, the reader cannot imagine the taciturn recluse ever revealing the nature of his love. Not until a veiled confession erupted with the last breaths his spirit forced from his lungs.

At the end of my secret love I, like Jean Valjean, faced life as a widower, without benefit of bell, book, candle . . . or bed. My initial taste of romantic love remained hidden of necessity from all but myself and God. The death of that inaugural relationship sent me into a spiral of bereavement, inflicting the most intense mental suffering I had ever known.

Fantine left the sorrowing Jean Valjean with a precious gift, her beloved Cosette. I could not see it at the time, but she whose loss I mourned left me with a timed-release treasure as precious as Fantine's child—the knowledge for the first time in my life of being desirable for myself, not for my status or accomplishments.

Harvesting the Depth and Richness of My Life

There is an Italian expression, *"Il prim' amore non si scorda mai"* ("One never forgets his or her first love"). What first-love memory does Jean Valjean's experience trigger in me? What traces of this relationship still linger at the edges of my spirit?

_____
_____
_____
_____
_____
_____
_____
_____
_____
_____

When has my heart been broken by a failed relationship? What long-term effect has this experience had on my life—whether positive or negative?

_____
_____
_____
_____
_____
_____
_____
_____
_____
_____

What did I learn from earlier relationships that prepared me for the one who is now my one true love?

_____
_____
_____
_____
_____
_____
_____
_____
_____
_____
_____
_____
_____

How have I dealt with my grief over lost or broken relationships? How willing have I been to give close friends and family healing access to my sorrow?

_____
_____
_____
_____
_____
_____
_____
_____
_____
_____
_____
_____
_____

Life Lessons

We Must Forgive Them

Those Thenardiers were wicked.
We must forgive them.

> Jean Valjean, Book Ninth, V:
> Night Behind Which is Dawn

ॐ

Reflection

I grew to maturity in a faith tradition that values for-giveness as a core virtue. Willingness to let go of past physical and psychological injuries and the hatreds they inspire was central to the teachings of Jesus of Nazareth. He did not invent forgiveness. He inherited it from his Hebrew religious tradition. The prophet Jeremiah put these words in God's mouth:

> I'll wipe the slate clean for each
> of them. I'll forget they ever
> sinned![1]

Echoing across three millennia, the prophet's living voice helps me to understand the kind of God we have—one for whom mere forgiveness of wrong-doing is insufficient. God does what I and most others find so difficult. God forgets that the sin ever occurred.[2]

Jesus lived this same spirit of unconditional forgive-ness to his dying breath: "Father, forgive them."[3] My complementary Judeo-Christian traditions call me to be-lieve that there is nothing I can do, no matter how despicable and horrendous, that God will not forgive—even forget.

Jean Valjean, the old fugitive, had a long list of peo-ple to forgive. There were judges who had sentenced him without consideration of mitigating factors. Inspec-tor Javert and others servants of the law had exerted upon him the cruelty of France's prison system.

The only common enemies father and daughter shared were the Thenardiers, the innkeepers who had bilked the desperate Fantine while subjecting her child

to slave-like conditions. Jean Valjean felt a special ur-
gency to assure his daughter that he had forgiven all
wrongs and she must do the same.

Though a Christ figure in Victor Hugo's immortal
novel, Jean Valjean was just a man. He carried to his
deathbed the hurtful memory of the innkeepers' unre-
pented wickedness. And who would blame Cosette for
hating the man and woman who had abused her as a
child and destroyed her mother's life? Still, her father
had delivered a clear mandate: "We"—not 'you,' notice,
but father and daughter together—"We must forgive
them."

Why did Jean Valjean insist on forgiveness? Why
should I forgive those who have "done me wrong"?
Stanford University professor Frederic Luskin, Ph.D.,
author of *Forgive for Good*,[4] offers a simple answer that his
critics dismiss as unrealistic and impractical. Forgiveness,
he says, is good for us!

> (Forgiveness) has been shown to
> reduce anger, hurt, depression and
> stress and lead to greater feelings of
> optimism, hope, compassion and
> self confidence.[5]

I take Luskin seriously, to the point that I have asked
myself often during the past several years, "Who else is
left for me to forgive?" My answer has been a consistent,
"No one."

Imagine my chagrin, when I awoke one recent morning with a virgin sun shining on a bitter, unforgiving
place in my heart. This cavern is so remote and rarely
visited that long stretches of my life have passed in de-
nial of its existence. The only way to access that place

and the ghosts who populate it is to ask myself: What is the one thing that would have made the greatest difference in the quality of my life, if someone had given me the compassionate guidance a young boy needed?

The answer embarrasses me, but here it is. If someone had assured me at age eleven of the normalcy of my emerging sexuality, my life for the next twenty years might have been quite different. Instead, those entrusted with the sacred duty of guiding me to adulthood offered a twisted morality. The potential for eternal damnation lurked in the closet of every sexual desire or experience.

A detailed recitation isn't appropriate here. What matters is that it took me most of my youthful adult years to arrive at the truth on my own. Along that journey to psychic and spiritual wholeness, I railed against a stadium-sized crowd of parents, nuns, clergy, teachers, other misguided adults.

Though I blamed these otherwise good people, they too had inherited centuries of unenlightened moral teaching and advice in the area of human sexuality. During my growing up years, the whole of Euro-American society reeled from the one-two punch of Protestant Puritanism[6] and Catholic Jansenism.[7] I place in evidence the motion picture industry code of ethics that allowed the comic team of Stan Laurel and Oliver Hardy to sleep in the same bed onscreen, but not a husband and wife. Traceable scars of my personal sexual conflict are migraine headaches that date from my late teens and remain unwelcome hangers-on to this day.

Over the years, I have worked to reconcile myself with my interior demons. But, just when I congratulate myself for having eradicated my bitterness through forgiveness, I am shocked by a new triggering event that reopens those still-raw wounds. This is most likely to occur today when someone I care about is stung by a remnant of that unreformed mindset. It happened recently when a friend in another state wished to join our faith community. When the local ecclesiastical "sex police" declared this exemplary person unfit (for reasons I am not at liberty to detail), all the rage I thought had been healed came flooding back.

I continue to feel bitter about my friend's treatment, and it would be easy—even in some dark way pleasurable—to wallow in righteous disgust. But, would I be happier? Would I be healthier for it? Would our wounded world be a better, safer place as a result? With due respect to my seething passions on this matter, I believe that Frederic Luskin, Victor Hugo, Jesus Christ, and all those wise and insightful men and women who inspired ("breathed life into") the great religious movements of human history are right. I hear them saying, "Those *&!#*@!*s were misguided or worse, but we must forgive them."

Harvesting the Depth and Richness of My Life

What one "true thing" do I wish I had learned earlier
in my life? What difference might it have made?

_____

_____

_____

_____

_____

_____

_____

_____

_____

_____

_____

_____

Who in my life, living or dead, still needs my forgiveness
—even if they may never know about it?

_____

_____

_____

_____

_____

_____

_____

_____

_____

_____

_____

_____

_____

_____

Scarcely Anything Else

Love each other dearly always. There is scarcely anything else in the world but that: to love one another.

Jean Valjean, Book Ninth, V:
Night Behind Which is Dawn

&

Reflection

Like many authors, I find it easier to write a complete manuscript than "pitch it" with a few summary, publisher-wowing words. Jean Valjean's success in reducing the whole of his life—everything he had learned and come to value and believe—into a pair of deathbed sentences gives me hope that I might do the same.[1] Not knowing when or how my end will come, I wrestle with the challenge of communicating to my daughters, in a capstone statement, everything I wish to bequeath from my life's experience.

Jean Valjean provides a model for my preparation. With the life light dimming in his eyes, he found at last the right combination of vowels and consonants and shaped them into words that echoed Jesus' "deathbed" gift to family and friends: "There is scarcely anything else in the world but that: to love one another."[2]

I wonder how long Jean Valjean had turned those climactic words on the potter's wheel of his spirit. I can't help but wonder, too, if he regretted at once their inevitable poverty. Might he have assembled a more eloquent and persuasive statement? He spoke of "love." But what is love, after all? Atrocities committed in its name litter world history and current events. Did Jean Valjean's dying counsel come close to embodying the "last word" on the meaning of life? Or, did death leave him with lingering frustration that he might have failed his daughter just when it mattered most, to both of them?

Reflecting on Jean Valjean's experience, perhaps I am burdening my life summary, when it surfaces, with unrealistic expectations. Who am I to think I can do better than the protégé of Bishop Charles-Francois-Bienvenu

Myriel? Yet, I keep reformulating—as in a secret "Last Words Laboratory"—what I will share with my daughters when I draw close to the end of this life. I imagine a priceless urn that future generations of hyphenated Garrottos [3] will treasure, but my potter's hands remain wet and caked with unset clay.

In the end, dramatic deathbed scenes may be nothing but a grand illusion. What if *Les Miserables* had ended with Jean Valjean dying unattended? What if the bishop's repentant thief had taken all his memories and hard-learned lessons unshared to his unmarked grave? [4] Would his daughter—and the novel's readers—have been impoverished for it. Hardly! Cosette's daily experience of her father had served as a lesson in the kind of enduring, unconditional love he counseled at the end.

Deathbeds are not meant for confession of long-withheld sins and belated sorrow for spousal or parental neglect. This happens and provides, I suppose, some consolation and healing when it does. The model Victor Hugo presents is that of a humble man who needed only to reprise at the end of his reformed life what he had demonstrated every day since his conversion at Digne.

Such is the lesson for this dad, too. I may utter my last words in a comfortable bed circled by my wife, daughters, grandchildren and closest family and friends. Or alone, perhaps on a sidewalk somewhere.

So, each day I do my best to make sure that the time and place will not matter. If I am unable to deliver my desired summation, I commission my life to proclaim it for me.

Harvesting the Depth and Richness of My Life

If I had but one brief moment to say goodbye (for the last time) to those closest to me, what would I say?

_____
_____
_____
_____
_____
_____
_____
_____
_____
_____
_____

Am I waiting for a deathbed scene (which I may not get) to resolve some unfinished issue with another person? What would it take to resolve this matter before I reach the unpredictable end of my life?

_____
_____
_____
_____
_____
_____
_____
_____
_____
_____
_____

In what way does something like a "Last Words Laboratory" exist within me? How might I describe this insight and its meaning?

_____

_____

_____

_____

_____

_____

_____

_____

_____

_____

_____

What summary message will I leave in legacy for my loved ones? How does it read today?

_____

_____

_____

_____

_____

_____

_____

_____

_____

_____

_____

*(Jean Valjean) had fallen
backwards, the light from the candlesticks
fell upon him; his white face looked up
towards heaven, he let Cosette and
Marius cover his hands with theirs; he
was dead.*

Jean Valjean, Book Ninth, V:
Night Behind Which is Dawn

℘

"One of my hopes in writing this book
is to inspire you to read
—if you have not done so—
the magnificent unabridged version of
Victor Hugo's Les Miserables
and come to love this timeless novel
as much as I do."

Alfred J. Garrotto

APPENDICES

1.

Diary Entry

May 17, 2006

Lord, in my not-yet-written book based on *Les Miser-ables*, I want to explore the importance of discovering one's true name: the name by which you know each of us. I can trace this through my life. Yet, I found in Thomas Merton's journals a passage in which he says that your name, YAHWEH, means: NO NAME.

If you have no name, why is it important for me to discern my true name? The light you have cast on this for me today, Father, is this: I must find the Self you created me to be and apply a *temporary* label to it. But, when I leave this world, I want to greet you, saying, "This is who I have been, whom you created me to be. Now, I offer that name to you."

So, it seems that we don't go into eternity as Alfred J. Garrotto, Author, or Abraham Lincoln, President, USA. We have no more need for a label to identify our Self-hood. We take the name YAHWEH (NO NAME)! You and I will be one, forever.

2.

Dad's First Hour

I spent my first hour as a dad in tears. During the months of our waiting, I had played with the fantasy of what the moment of first encounter with my daughter would be like . . . how I would feel, how she would respond to me. I had gone over every possible scenario, but I hadn't prepared myself for what actually happened.

Esther and I had taken the PanAm "red eye" from San Francisco to San Salvador, El Salvador (via Los Angeles and Guatemala City). On arrival at the heavily guarded international airport, we felt weary enough to sleep and wired awake with anticipation. Silvia, our driver and guide, offered us the alternatives of going to our hotel to freshen up or to Hogar del Niño, the orphanage, to see our daughter.

Guess which we chose?

Hogar del Niño is in a part of the city particularly devastated by the earthquake of October 1986. Directly across the street, collapsing walls had crushed fifteen children as they waited outside their school for their rides. A year later, evidence of the quake littered the neighborhood. The orphanage itself showed ugly, unhealed wounds. Yet, the Vincentian Sisters and lay staff carried on the daily task of caring for the physical, emotional and spiritual needs of 580 children, ages birth to eighteen.

From the moment we entered the grounds, I sensed we were on holy ground—a shrine in which the sacred objects were not relics of dead saints. Living saints inhabited these premises, displaced by a civil war not of their making, by the death of parents, or by the sad-eyed, hollow-bellied hopelessness of poverty.

Unused to Latin American ways, we expected someone to bring our daughter to us in a private parlor where we could begin the process of getting acquainted. Things didn't happen that way in an environment where privacy was a luxury and people lived life's most intimate moments in the presence of others. One of the Sisters escorted us into a back yard where dozens of children milled about on the dusty, broken concrete.

In a crowd of curious eyes, two appeared bigger, blacker and more wonder-filled than the others. No laughter brightened those eyes, just as we had seen no humor in the little girl whose photos we had treasured for the past five months. Her round face was solemn. Aware that the moment of election had arrived, she doubted she wanted to be the chosen one that day.

Esther spotted Monica first. "Look, Al, it's her!"

My throat swelled and went dry. I gazed down at a tiny beauty dressed in a once-white smock that radiated the noonday Salvadoran sun and contrasted with her olive complexion. While I fumbled with my camera to capture this life-changing moment, Monica consented to her election and melded her body into Esther's embrace. She belonged to us! We had arrived at "the first day of the rest of our lives."

Before I could take my own sweet little girl into my arms, another child a few feet away caught my attention.

She had broken into a low-pitched keening that echoed off the adobe walls surrounding the courtyard.

"This is Blanca Estela," the kind nun informed me, "her sister."

To my surprise, the child held in her hands the photo of Esther and me, which we had sent to Monica months earlier. We had learned of our daughter's seven-year-old half-sister only days before leaving for El Salvador. She too, the nun told us, awaited adoption by American parents, who would come for her soon. Blanca knew we had come to take her sister away—and thought it must be forever.

How was this possible, I asked myself? We would never have wanted such a cruel encounter to take place.

Though I longed to meet and hold my new daughter, I felt compelled to embrace and console the inconsolable child. In my arms she begged to come with us so she and her sister could remain together. In my cobbled Spanish and choking back sobs of my own, I pledged to do everything in my power to reunite the sisters in the United States.[1]

I suspected that Blanca had been told too many lies to place much faith in the word of a stranger.

Welcome to parenthood!

3.

Dad's Longest Day

The longest day of my life occurred on the shortest day of the year—December 21, 1988. I had traveled to Tegucigalpa, Honduras, three days earlier. My wife stayed behind with our first child, adopted only a year before in El Salvador. We hated being separated for this big event, but it had to be.

After several days of waiting, I finally had clearance to bring our three-year-old daughter, Cristina Elena, home to the United States.

The night before our departure, neither Cristina nor I got any sleep. She refused to stay in the crib, insisting instead on cuddling with her new dad. Her lingering diarrhea complicated the morning. We had a full day of flying ahead of us, including a final customs interview in Houston. I looked forward to the trip with both excitement and dread.

I always wondered what that day meant to Cristina. I found out when she wrote the following poem at age 15.

Never Shall I Forget

by

Cristina E. Garrotto

Never shall I forget
the day that changed my life forever,
the day that made me so excited and so scared
at the same time.

Never shall I forget
my father, the new man in my life,
whom I would look up to.

Never shall I forget
when my father took me to the airport
where it all started.
I wouldn't go up the stairs, but I wouldn't walk away.

Never shall I forget
the way I felt that very moment.
My whole life was going to change in a second if I was to
get on that plane.
I didn't know if it would change in a good way
or in a bad way.
I had to trust the man who was leading me there,
that it was going to be fine,
that I wouldn't have to worry.
He grabbed me up into his arms and we were off.

Never shall I forget
how nervous I was during the flight.
I had the jitters all the way.

I would not leave my father's lap.
He held me all the way there.
It was nearly Christmas and as we entered California,
all I could see were the most beautiful colorful lights,
"*Las luces!*"

Never shall I forget,
as I entered, that I saw the most beautiful ladies
I had ever seen.
We were walking towards them.
I was being held in my father's arms,
whom I had trusted with my life.

Never shall I forget
when I heard that these two people were part
of my new family.

Never shall I forget
the smile on my new mother's face.
How happy she was to finally see me again.
And it was the same for me too.
I walked into her arms
and she placed her arms around me.
Just the feeling of her arms around me,
I knew that she was going to take good care of me.

Never shall I forget
the way my new sister looked at me
with her big brown eyes,
such a gentle look, coming towards me.
I was scared at first.

Never shall I forget
the way she picked me up. I was not happy.

I pushed her away.
I guess because I was scared
and had never seen this person,
that already she might do something bad to me.

Never shall I forget
that day and night that changed my life forever,
the night that led me to the perfect family.

Never shall I forget
their faces which lit up my heart with joy,
the faces I could not take my eyes off.

Never shall I forget
the beauty of their smiles which made me
want to smile.

Never shall I forget
the smell of happiness that would be with me forever.

Never shall I forget
the arms that held me so tight,
the first time I had ever felt so safe in my whole life.

Never shall I forget
the touch of their cheeks, the first time
that I had placed my lips upon theirs.

Never shall I forget
their voices—the sound of music.

Never shall I forget
the beating of my heart, which wouldn't stop
when I fixed my eyes upon my beautiful future family.

NOTES

Page numbers attached to quotations from *Les Miserables*, reference the Modern Library edition (undated).

Introduction

1. *The Temptation of the Impossible: Victor Hugo and* Les Miserables, Mario Vargas Llosa, pages 176-177, 2004, Princeton University Press.
2. Iranian-born Michele Roohani is as wise as she is talented. Her inspirational photographs and writings (on a wide range of topics) are found at http://www.micheleroohani.com/.

In Search of Wisdom

A Distant Horizon

1. "(The Lord) told me: My grace is enough; it's all you need. My strength comes into its own in your weakness," 2 Corinthians 12:10. *The Message*, translation of the Bible by Eugene Peterson
2. Fantine, Book Fourth, VI: Father Fauchelevent (145-147)

The Phantom Promise

Introduction

1.   Fantine, Book Second, VI: Jean Valjean (73)
2.   This core theme of Victor Hugo's novel reflects the parable Jesus told as a way of shedding light on what is meant by the "kingdom of heaven." A king forgave his servant an enormous debt. The man went right out and extorted payment from one of his own debtors who owed him a tiny amount. Dismayed when he learned of his beneficiary's insensitivity, the king said: "I forgave your entire debt . . . . Shouldn't you be compelled to be merciful to your fellow servant?"
Matthew 18:32. *The Message*, translation of the Bible by Eugene Peterson

I Am Purchasing Your Soul

1.   An echo of: "Jesus sent his twelve harvest hands out with this charge: 'Go to the lost, confused people right here in the neighborhood. Tell them that the kingdom is here. Bring health to the sick. Raise the dead. Touch the untouchables. Kick out the demons. You have been treated generously, so live generously,' " Matthew 10:6-8. *The Message*, translation of the Bible by Eugene Peterson
2.   Fantine, Book Second, XIII: Petite Gervais (94)
3.   Fantine, Book Second, XIII: Petite Gervais (94-95)

les miserables

Introduction

1.   Book of Amos 2:6-16

Raise the Drawbridge

1. From "The Great Colossus" by Emma Lazarus
2. Asian immigrants generally entered the United States through Angel Island in San Francisco Bay.

Justice Trumps Mercy

1. Charity here is synonymous with mercy, or caring for the immediate needs of another person.
2. Justice here means working for the creation of institutions and laws that honor fundamental human rights and promote the common good.
3. The context of Jean Valjean's taking or accepting the name Madeleine in the novel would not seem to be as a "convert from sin" (the common but erroneous attribution given to Mary of Magdala). The citizens of Montreuil-sur-Mer had no knowledge of Jean Valjean's past. Did they confer the name, or did Jean Valjean assume it himself? Hugo is vague on this point—at least in Charles E. Wilbour's 1862 English translation. He uses the passive voice: "He was known from that time by the name of Father Madeleine," Fantine, Book Fifth, II: Madeleine (134).
4. Fantine, Book Fifth, II: Madeleine (134-135)

The Primacy of Conscience

Introduction

1. Fantine, Book Second, XIII: Petit Gervais (90-96)

Compass of the Unknown

1. Fantine, Book Eighth, III: A Tempest in a Brain (190-191)

Go In Peace

1. Matthew 4:9, *The Message,* translation of the Bible by Eugene Peterson
2. Fantine, Book Seventh, III: A Tempest in the Brain (192)
3. Jean Valjean, Book Sixth, IV: Immortale Jecur (1160)

The Violence of Thought

1. Jean Valjean, Book Fourth, I: Javert Off the Track (1106)

My Name is Jean Valjean

A Name Too Small

1. Dr. Brian Swimme is Director of the Center for the Story of the Universe in San Francisco, CA (www.brianswimme.org). His books include *The Hidden Heart of the Cosmos: Humanity and the New Story* and *The Universe is a Green Dragon: A Cosmic Creation Story.*
2. Saint Denis, Book Third, IV: Change of Grating (750)
3. Jean Valjean, Book Ninth, V: Night Behind Which is Dawn (1221)

A Name is a Centre

1. William Shakespeare, *Romeo and Juliet* (II, ii, 1-2)

2. *Saint Denis, Book Seventh, II: Roots* (836)

3. Exodus 3:13, *The Message*, translation of the Bible by Eugene Peterson

4. Exodus 3:14, *The Message*, translation by Eugene Peterson

5. Isaiah 43:1, *The Message*, translation by Eugene Peterson

6. Matthew 10:29-30, *The Message*, translation by Eugene Peterson

7. Cf. Martin Buber's: "I / it" vs. "I / thou."

8. During a second nine-month imprisonment in 1823, Jean Valjean wore the number 9430. Cosette, Book Second, III: Showing That the Chain of the Iron Ring Must Needs Have Undergone a Certain Preparation to be Thus Broken by One Blow of the Hammer (316)

A Name is a Me

1. It is ironic that Jean Valjean's original "crime" involved theft of a simple loaf of bread.

2. Father Fauchelevent was the man M. Madeleine (Jean Valjean) had rescued from being trapped under a collapsed cart in Montreuil-sur-Mer.

3. "The mother (superior) added: 'He is Father Fauvent's brother.' In fact, Jean Valjean was regularly installed; he had the leather kneecap and the bell; henceforth he had his commission. His name was Ultimus Fauchelevent." Cosette, Book Eighth, VIII: Successful Examination (478).

4. Jean Valjean to Marius: ". . . suddenly you hear a voice shout this name: Jean Valjean! and you see that appalling hand, the police, spring out of the shadow and abruptly tear off my mask." Jean Valjean, Book Seventh, I: The Seventh Circle and the Eighth Heaven (1170)

5. Jean Valjean, Book Seventh, I: The Seventh Circle and the Eighth Heaven (1169)
6. I have written most of my novels under the name A. J. Garrotto.
7. Joseph William Garrotto and Josephine Concetta Alesio. I use Mom's middle name here with some guilt. She despised the name and never used it—only the initial 'C' at times.
8. "(Cosette) called him Father, and knew him by no other name." Saint Denis, Book III, II: Jean Valjean a National Guard, 743. See also, Cosette, Book Fourth, IV: What the Landlady Discovered (372-373)

Shock and Awe of Parenthood

A Heart Full of Freshness (1)

1. In Appendix 2, see the reprint of my article, "Dad's First Hour." The incidents described took place earlier in the day of our first night together with Monica.

A Heart Full of Freshness (2)

1. See "Dad's Longest Day" and "Never Shall I Forget," in Appendix 3.

The Primal Wound

1. Verrier, Nancy Newton, The Primal Wound, Gateway Press, Inc.
2. Verrier, Nancy Newton, The Primal Wound, Page xvi

A Gift in the Present Tense

1. Fantine, Book Fifth, VI: Father Fauchelevent (147)
2. William Shakespeare, *Hamlet*, Hamlet's soliloquy

The Power of Story

Bedtime Stories

1. "O God, lover of all life, who stands watch over the birds of the air . . ." I cannot remember the rest of the prayer, although I am sure I have it written down somewhere.

Lost Angels

1. Jean Valjean knew nothing of his foreman's action—setting up a classic case of "The buck stops here."

A Father's Farewell: The Last Words of Jean Valjean

Introduction

1. The wedding took place on February 16, 1833—Mardi Gras, the day before Ash Wednesday.
2. Jean Valjean, Book Seventh, I: The Seventh Circle and the Eighth Heaven (1164)
3. Jean Valjean, Book Seventh, I: The Seventh Circle and the Eighth Heaven (1165)

4. Jean Valjean, Book Seventh, I: The Seventh Circle and the Eighth Heaven (1174-1175)
5. Jean Valjean, Book Ninth, I: Pity for the Unhappy, But Indulgence for the Happy (1195)

Memories

To Me They are Gold

1. Fantine, Book Second, XIII: Petite Gervais (94-95).
2. Reading beyond the author's text, we can only speculate about how many times the bishop had lost this bet on similar throws of the dice. Also, there is no record in the novel that Jean Valjean ever saw or communicated with his benefactor again. Hugo tells us that, upon reading of the bishop's death in 1821, Jean Valjean "dressed in black with crepe on his hat" Fantine, Book Fifth, IV: Monsieur Madeleine in Mourning (139). When asked the reason for his mourning this obscure bishop, he responded, "In my youth, I was a servant in his family" (141).
3. "This . . . happened with (Jean Valjean) from time to time, at very long intervals. He remained absent for one or two days at the most. Where did he go? nobody knew, not even Cosette . . . . It was generally when money was needed for the household expenses that Jean Valjean made these little journeys." Saint Denis, Book Fifth, II: Fears of Cosette (779)

Is He Pleased With Me?

1. "Good work! You did your job well." Matthew 25:21, The Parable of the Talents, *The Message*, translation of the Bible by Eugene Peterson

2. Jean Valjean, Book Ninth, V: Night Behind Which is Dawn (1220)

Secret Love

1. Cosette, Book Fourth, III: Two Misfortunes Mingled Make Happiness (371)

Life Lessons

We Must Forgive Them

1. Jeremiah 31:33-34: "This is a brand-new covenant that I will make with Israel when the time comes. I will put my law within them—write it on their hearts!—and be their God. And they will be my people. They will no longer go around setting up schools to teach each other about God. They'll know me firsthand, the dull and the bright, the smart and the slow. I'll wipe the slate clean for each of them. I'll forget they ever sinned!" (underline added). *The Message*, translation of the Bible by Eugene Peterson

2. In his deeply spiritual poem, *"Dieu: La Lumière"* ("God: The Light-Source"), 1855, Victor Hugo says of God: "Not 'vengeful,' not 'forgiving'—his eternal kiss takes no notice of the bite."—*Selected Poems of Victor Hugo*, Translated by E. H. and A. M. Blackmore, University of Chicago Press, paperback edition, 2004.

3. Luke 23:34

4. *Forgive for Good*, Harper Collins, 2002. Fred Luskin, Ph.D., is the Co-Director of the Stanford-Northern Ireland HOPE Project, an ongoing series of workshops and research projects that investigate the effectiveness of his forgiveness methods on the victims of political violence.

He served as the Director of the Stanford Forgiveness Project, the largest research project to date on the training and measurement of a forgiveness intervention. He is currently a Senior Fellow at the Stanford Center on Conflict and Negotiation.

5. Text retrieved February 23, 2008 from Dr. Luskin's website at http://www.learningtoforgive.com/about.htm.

6. In modern usage, the word *puritan* is used as an informal pejorative for someone who has strict views on sexual morality, disapproves of recreation, and wishes to impose these beliefs on others. The popular image is slightly more accurate as a description of Puritans in colonial America, who were among the most radical Puritans and whose social experiment took the form of a Calvinist theocracy. (Source: Wikipedia at http://en.wikipedia.org/wiki/Puritan).

7. Jansenism, named after Flemish bishop Cornelis Jansen, was a Roman Catholic reform movement in Europe during the 17th and 18th centuries. Taken to its extreme, Jansenism maintained that human nature is incapable of good and salvation is limited only to those predestined to it. Although these teachings were condemned as heretical by the Roman Catholic Church, the spirit of Jansenism became embedded in Catholic practice throughout Western Europe and the British Isles. Waves of immigrants brought it to America during the late nineteenth and early twentieth centuries.

Scarcely Anything Else

1. In Boublil and Schonberg's stage/musical version of *Les Miserables*, lyricist Herbert Kretzmer rendered Hugo's

words as: "To love one another is to see the face of God."

2. John 13:34: "I give you a new commandment: Love one another. Such as my love has been for you, so must your love be for each other. This is how all will know you for my disciples: your love for one another," *New American Bible*, Catholic Book Publishing Company, 1972.

3. I am the last male in our branch of the Garrotto bloodline. My daughters, if they choose to marry, may or may not wish to carry and pass on their (hyphenated) surname. The question of bloodline meant a lot to my father. It has been of little import to me. At an early age I opted for a celibate lifestyle. In marriage we chose to adopt. I prefer my daughters to display who I am in the spiritual and emotional quality of their lives—rather than in the way they sign their names.

4. "This stone is entirely blank . . . . No name can be read there." Jean Valjean, Book Ninth, V: Night Behind Which is Dawn (1222)

Appendices

2.   *Dad's First Hour*

1. Several families, including our own, have tried over the years to adopt Blanca. As far as I know, she never left El Salvador. She would now a young woman in her mid-20s.

3.   *Dad's Longest Day*

"Never Shall I Forget" by Cristina E. Garrotto (© 2000 by Cristina E. Garrotto). She arrived from Honduras on December 21, 1988, less than a month before her fourth birthday.

About the Author

The Wisdom of Les Miserables is Alfred J. Garrotto's fourth book-length nonfiction work. It follows *Christ in Our Lives, Christians and Prayer,* and *Christians Reconciling* (Winston Press, St Paul, MN). Most recently he has focused on fiction, authoring five novels. In his capacity as lay minister in a large suburban parish, he coordinates adult faith formation, bereavement and lector ministries and is available for spiritual direction.

Born in Santa Monica, California, he now resides and writes in the San Francisco Bay Area where he is active in the Mount Diablo Branch of the California Writers Club.

Wisdom Workshops and Retreats

Alfred J. Garrotto is available to groups for workshops and retreats. He offers a variety of formats tailored to each organization's needs and preferences. Options range from a half-day (or evening) to three days (or a weekend). Groups may choose from a six-part program (below) based on the major themes of *The Wisdom of Les Miserables: Lessons From the Heart of Jean Valjean.*

Series 1—*In Search of Wisdom*

Series 2—*The Primacy of Conscience*

Series 3—*My Name is Jean Valjean*

Series 4—*Shock and Awe of Parenthood*

Series 5—*The Power of Story*

Series 6—*Last Words of Jean Valjean*

Individual Wisdom Mentoring

The author offers one-on-one mentoring in the art of wise living. Options include in-person sessions, phone and e-mail.

For information about
workshop, retreat, and individual options,
contact *algarrotto@comcast.net.*

Visit Alfred J. Garrotto on the Web at

www.blsinc.com/garrotto.htm

and

www.authorsden.com/alfredjgarrottohtm

Novels by A. J. Garrotto

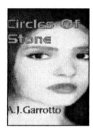

Circles of Stone A-List model Natalia McCrory is on the verge of an emotional breakdown. Her journey to love, spiritual peace, and the meaning of her existence is told with great serenity and insight. (Hilliard & Harris, 2003, paperback and hard cover).

Down a Narrow Alley continues Natalia McCrory's life journey. The abandonment of 10-yr.-old Marisol at a Lima orphanage sets in motion a sequence of events the reader will ponder long after turning the final page. (Lulu Press, 2007, paperback)

I'll Paint a Sun A month before their Valentine's Day wedding, Libby O'Neill's fiancé and business partner walks out—taking all their money with him. Plunged into despair, Libby cannot foresee that God is about to send her an angel in disguise. (Genesis Press, Inc./ Kensington, 2005, paperback).

Finding Isabella Analisa Marconi's adoptive parents perish in a plane crash that she alone survives. Devastated and now rootless, she returns to her native country to search for her birth mother and any siblings. (Genesis Press, Inc., 2000, paperback).

Available through Amazon.com and other major online book sellers

May all your storms be weathered,
all that's good get better.

"Here's to Life"
Joe Galt